BUT WAS IT
JUST?

BUT WAS IT

JUST?

REFLECTIONS ON THE MORALITY
OF
THE PERSIAN GULF WAR

JEAN BETHKE ELSHTAIN
STANLEY HAUERWAS
SARI NUSSEIBEH
MICHAEL WALZER
GEORGE WEIGEL

with an Appendix from *La Civiltà Cattolica*
Translated by Peter Heinegg

Edited by
DAVID E. DECOSSE

Doubleday

NEW YORK LONDON TORONTO SYDNEY AUCKLAND

PUBLISHED BY DOUBLEDAY
a division of Bantam Doubleday Dell Publishing Group, Inc.
666 Fifth Avenue, New York, New York 10103

DOUBLEDAY and the portrayal of an anchor with a dolphin are trademarks of
Doubleday, a division of Bantam Doubleday Dell Publishing Group, Inc.

Book design by Patrice Fodero

Library of Congress Cataloging-in-Publication Data

But was it just? : reflections on the morality of the Persian Gulf War /
Jean Bethke Elshtain . . . [et al.] ; with an appendix from La civiltà cattolica
translated by Peter Heinegg; edited by David E. DeCosse.
p.   cm.
1. Persian Gulf War, 1991—Moral and ethical aspects.   2. Persian Gulf War,
1991—Religious aspects.   3. Just war doctrine.   I. Elshtain, Jean Bethke,
1941–   .   II. DeCosse, David E.
DS79.72.B88   1992
956.704′3—dc20   91-35693
CIP
ISBN: 0-385-42281-4

CONTENTS

EDITOR'S NOTE

This book has two goals. The first is to evaluate President George Bush's claim that the Persian Gulf War was just. The second is to bring to the widest possible audience a sustained discussion of the morality of the war.

One year ago the war ended in an allied rout of Iraqi forces. Shortly after, on March 6, 1991, President Bush told a joint session of Congress, "We went halfway around the world to do what is moral, just, and right." His moral claim before Congress capped months of unprecedented ethical talk by the President, the media, religious leaders, intellectuals, and working men and women. Ancient and medieval names flew over airwaves and satellite dishes as figures like Augustine of Hippo and Thomas Aquinas were invoked in the search for establishing the justice or injustice of the war.

It is never easy to assess moral claims made by a politician. Are they to be taken at face value? Or are they a smoke screen meant to obscure some backstage manipulation of events? Furthermore, if these claims are taken at face value, how is it that they have been arrived at? Is it simply an instinctive sense that an action, like the defense of an invaded country, is right? Or are there canons of justice that explain the reasoning behind moral claims and provide means for evaluating these claims?

This book contains reflections on these questions by five leading ethical writers on war and peace; it also contains an editorial prompted by the Gulf War that appears to signal a significant shift in thought by the Catholic Church on matters of war and peace. Michael Walzer, whose essay "Justice and Injustice in the Gulf War" opens the volume, is the UPS Foundation Professor of Social Science at the Institute for Advanced Study in Princeton, New Jersey. His essay focuses on the justness—indeed the obligation—of opposing aggression like Saddam Hussein's invasion of Kuwait.

George Weigel, the president of the Ethics and Public Policy Center in Washington, D.C., argues in his essay, "From Last Resort to Endgame: Morality, the Gulf War, and the Peace Process," that the war conformed classically to centuries-old criteria for what makes a war just; he also explores how the war affected Middle East prospects for peace.

Jean Bethke Elshtain, Centennial Professor of Political Science at Vanderbilt University in Nashville, Tennessee, also takes up traditional just war thinking in her essay, "Just War as Politics: What the Gulf War Told Us About Contemporary American Life." Her conclusions, however, are critical of the conduct of the war. Moreover, she also considers the role of women in the Gulf in light of just war thinking.

In "Can Wars Be Just? A Palestinian Viewpoint of the Gulf War," Sari Nusseibeh argues against the justness of the war from a unique vantage point: the inside of an Israeli jail. Nusseibeh, a Palestinian political leader and specialist in Islamic philosophy, was arrested at his East Jerusalem home on January 29, 1991, and charged with providing Iraqi authorities with information on the landing of Scud missiles then being fired at Israel. Nusseibeh has vehemently denied the charge and has never been allowed to see the evidence for it. After three months in jail, he was released and is now director of the Jerusalem Center for Strategic Research.

Stanley Hauerwas is Professor of Theological Ethics at Duke University in Durham, North Carolina, and a Christian pacifist. In "Whose Just War? Which Peace?" he argues that the just war theory invoked by the President and others in support of the war was a cover story for an immoral military campaign based on power politics and crusading patriotism.

In Appendix One, the editors of *La Civiltà Cattolica,* a Jesuit magazine in Rome which has its editorials reviewed by the Vatican Secretariat of State, say that the day of just war theory is all but over. The Gulf War, they say, has again testified to the vast destructiveness and lack of control inherent in modern war; these tendencies, the editors say, have pushed aside the controls of just war tenets, making them increasingly obsolete. That such a judgment appears in a publication with quasi-official status at the Vatican could signal a new direction in the thought of the Roman Catholic Church, which for centuries has been the leading articulator in the West of the just war tradition.

In Appendix Two, a chronology of the Gulf crisis is provided. The chronology highlights those events and statements which bear particularly on the question of the war's justness.

At a time when political discourse is moribund and moral discussion is paralyzed by sloganeering, these essays are models of forceful, reasoned argument. Their points of view vary; their conclusions differ. In aiming to bring this ethical discussion to a wide audience, we hope that the cogency of these writers will allow readers more easily to make up their minds about the justness of the war, and to be readier to assess the morality of conflicts that are sure to come.

I would like to thank the contributors for the remarkable spirit, clarity, and insight of their essays. I would also like to thank Tom Cahill, Mike Iannazzi, Alicia DiLeo and Nancy Haught for their help in putting the volume together.

David E. DeCosse
New York, New York

JUSTICE AND INJUSTICE IN THE GULF WAR

MICHAEL WALZER

I

Political theories are tested by events in the political world. We ask whether the theory illuminates the events. Does it bring the right issues into relief? Is it helpful in shaping, justifying, and explaining our moral responses and judgments?

During the last fifteen years, there has been a significant revival of just war theory—driven, as my own writing has been, largely by the Vietnam experience. Many books and articles have been published, many courses taught, not only in liberal arts colleges but also in the U.S. military academies. The language of just war theory has appeared increasingly in public discussions—first in the debates about nuclear deterrence, then in the wider debate that preceded the war in the Persian Gulf. Indeed, it has been adopted by our political and military leaders (a small example: the designation of the 1989 Panama invasion as Operation Just Cause, which it probably wasn't). This is a dangerous moment for any theory. Think of the perverse if exhilarating effects upon religion whenever the language of holiness is taken over by politicians. Of course, politics and war are never holy, not, at least, as I understand holiness, while they are sometimes, or to some degree, just. But only sometimes and to some degree, and when more blanket justifications are claimed, the theory is rendered suspect. If it can be used to defend injustice, should it be used at all?

In fact, whether or not its specific terminology is adopted, just war theory has always played a part in official arguments about war. No political leader can send soldiers into battle, ask them to risk their lives and to kill other people, without assuring them that their cause is just—and that of their enemies unjust. And if the theory is used, it is also, inevitably, misused. Sometimes, it serves only to determine what lies our leaders tell, the complex structure of their hypocrisy, the tribute that vice pays to virtue. But the theory is always available for alternative service. It can also play a critical role, grounding and specifying the demand for a more honorable tribute. So it is important not to give up the theory just because of its misuse—any more than we would give up our ideas about friendship just because they are exploited by false friends. We need a systematic account of justice to help us make choices and distinctions, to prepare us for political decision-making or for the more ordinary work of criticizing (or supporting) this or that war or wartime decision.

II

Consider the war in the Persian Gulf as a test case. Conscripted into service, how well did the theory serve? Curi-

2

ously, some critics of the war, particularly religious critics (some Catholic bishops, the leaders of the World Council of Churches), tried simultaneously to use and discard the theory. They talked about justice because they wanted to say that the war was unjust, and they discarded much of the theory of justice because they were afraid (or, better, acutely aware) that, in standard just war terms, it wasn't. They commonly ended up with an argument that seems to me both dangerous and wrong: that no war in the modern world can possibly be just. The theory for them has lost its capacity to make distinctions. Given the resources of a modern army, given the availability of weapons of mass destruction, the old categories can't do any serious work. We are left with a theory of justice that is obsolete and a practice of war that is obscene.

It is certainly possible to reinterpret or reconstruct just war theory so that no war could possibly be justified. It is important to stress, however, that "no war" here means *no war past or present.* The most massively destructive form of warfare is also one of the oldest: the siege of a city, in which the civilian population is the avowed target and no effort is made to single out soldiers and military bases for attack—one of the classic requirements of justice in war. Those opponents of the Gulf War who advocated a prolonged blockade of Iraq seem not to have realized that what they were advocating was a radically indiscriminate act of war, with predictably harsh consequences. Just war theory as I understand it would require that food and medical supplies be let through—but in that case it is unlikely that the blockade would serve its purpose. In any case, we have no reason to think that judgments of this sort are any more difficult now than they were hundreds or thousands of years ago. There never was a golden age of warfare when just war categories were easy to apply and therefore regularly applied. If anything, modern technology makes it possible to fight with greater discrimination now than in the past, if there is a political will to do so.

Nonetheless, it is possible to construe the theory so that discrimination between military and civilian targets becomes irrelevant. And then, as we will see, another distinction is also lost: between just war theory and pacifism. Some of the bishops, though still formally committed to the just war, seem to me to have moved in this direction. The move involves a new stress upon two maxims of the theory: first, that war must be a "last resort," and second, that its anticipated costs to soldiers and civilians alike must not be disproportionate to (greater than) the value of its ends. I do not think that either maxim helps us much in making the moral distinctions that we need to make. And the Gulf War provides a useful illustration of the inadequacy of the two.

I will begin with the sequence of events. Iraq invaded Kuwait in early August 1990; Kuwaiti resistance was brief and ineffective, and the country was occupied in a matter of days. That was the beginning, and might have been the end, of the war. There ensued a brief flurry of diplomatic activity, against a background of American mobilization and the arrival of U.S. troops in Saudi Arabia. The diplomacy produced an economic blockade of Iraq, sanctioned by the United Nations and militarily enforced by a coalition of states led and dominated by the United States. Though the blockade required very little military enforcement, it was technically and practically an act of war. But the common perception during those months (August 1990–January 1991) was that the Gulf was at peace, while the coalition tried to reverse the Iraqi aggression without violence and debated, in slow motion and cold blood, whether or not to begin the war. It was in the context of this debate that the question of "last resort" was posed.

Had the Kuwaiti army, against all the odds, succeeded in holding off the invaders for a few weeks or months, the question would never have arisen. War would have been the first resort of the Kuwaitis, acceptably so given the immediacy and violence of the invasion, and any allied or friendly state could legitimately have joined in their defense. The failure of the resistance opened a kind of temporal and moral hiatus during which it was possible to seek alternative resolutions of the conflict. The blockade was merely one of many alternatives, which included United Nations condemnation of Iraq, its diplomatic and political isolation, various degrees of economic sanction, and a negotiated settlement involving small or large concessions to the aggressor. The actual blockade might have taken different forms, adapted to different ends; the coalition might, for example, have aimed at the containment rather than the reversal of Iraqi aggression.

I assume that it was morally obligatory to canvass these possibilities and to weigh their likely consequences. But it is hard to see how it could have been obligatory to adopt one of them, or a sequence of them, simply so that war would be a "last resort." If the allies, weighing the consequences of the alternatives, one of which was the continued occupation of Kuwait, had decided on an early (September, say) ultimatum—withdraw or face a counterattack—the decision would not have been unjust. They would have had to allow a decent interval for the withdrawal to be considered and its modalities negotiated, and we would want some assurance that they had good reasons to think that other strategies would not work or would work only at great cost to the people of Kuwait. Given the interval and the reasons, the doctrine of "last resort" doesn't seem to play any important role here.

Taken literally, which is exactly the way many people took it during the months of the blockade, "last resort" would make war morally impossible. For we can never reach lastness, or we can never know that we have reached

5

it. There is always something else to do: another diplomatic note, another United Nations resolution, another meeting. Once something like a blockade is in place, it is always possible to wait a little longer and hope for the success of (what looks like but isn't quite) nonviolence. Assuming, however, that war was justified in the first instance, at the moment of the invasion, then it is justifiable at *any* subsequent point when its costs and benefits seem on balance better than those of the available alternatives.

But sending troops into battle commonly brings with it so many unanticipated costs that it has come to represent a moral threshold: political leaders must cross this threshold only with great reluctance and trepidation. This is the truth contained in the "last resort" maxim. If there are potentially effective ways of avoiding actual fighting while still confronting the aggressor, they should be tried. In the hiatus months of the Gulf crisis, it seems to me that they were tried. The combination of economic blockade, military threat, and diplomatic deadline was a strategy plausibly designed to bring about an Iraqi withdrawal. Politics and war commonly work on timetables of this sort. Our blockade of Iraq was not a conventional siege, to be maintained until mass starvation forced Saddam Hussein's surrender. We were committed and, as I have already said, should have been committed to let food and medical supplies through before people started dying in the streets—though many people would have died anyway from the longer-term effects of malnutrition and disease. The blockade was aimed above all at Iraq's military-industrial capacity. But Saddam could have let this capacity run down over a period of months or even years, so long as he was sure that he wouldn't be attacked. Hence, the blockade's effectiveness depended on a credible threat to fight, and this threat, once it was mounted, could not be sustained indefinitely. At some point, the Iraqis had to yield or the coalition had to fight. If

6

they didn't yield and it didn't fight, the victory would have been theirs: aggression triumphant. Most competent observers, applying this or that version of rational decision theory, expected Iraq to yield before the January 15 deadline. When that did not happen, war was, though not a "last," surely a legitimate resort.

But at this point the proportionality maxim is brought into play, and it is argued that war can never be legitimate under modern conditions because its costs will always be greater than its benefits. Certainly, we want political and military leaders to worry about costs and benefits. But they have to *worry;* they can't calculate, for the values at stake are not commensurate—at least they can't be expressed or compared mathematically, as the idea of proportion suggests. How do we measure the value of a country's independence against the value of the lives that might be lost in defending it? How do we figure in the value of defeating an aggressive regime (the invasion of Kuwait was not the first, nor was it likely to be the last, of Iraq's aggressions) or the value of deterring other, similar regimes? All values of this latter sort are likely to lose out to the body count, since it is only bodies that can be counted. And then it is impossible to fight any wars except those that promise to be bloodless, and not only on one side. This last is an entirely respectable position—pacifism, not just war—but anyone holding it will have to recognize and accept the nonpacific results of trying to accommodate states like Saddam Hussein's Iraq.

At the same time, no sane political leader would choose a war that brought millions or even hundreds of thousands of deaths, or that threatened the world with nuclear destruction, for the sake of Kuwaiti independence. This is the truth in the proportionality maxim. But it is a gross truth, and while it will do some work in cases like the Soviet Union's 1968 invasion of Czechoslovakia (no one proposed that the United States mobilize for a military response), it isn't going

7

to make for useful discriminations in the greater number of cases. Most of the time, we can make only short-term predictions, and we have no way that even mimics mathematics of comparing the costs of fighting to the costs of not fighting, since one set of costs is necessarily speculative, while the other comes in, as it were, over an indeterminate time span. If we simply insist in advance that, given the weapons currently available, fighting is sure to produce catastrophic losses, the proportionality maxim would indeed rule out war in this and every other case: but this proposition is false.

We have to ask instead which particular weapons are likely to be used, how they will be used, and for what ends. About all these matters, just war theory has a great deal to say, and what it has to say is importantly restrictive. When it comes to resisting aggression, by contrast, the theory is at least permissive, sometimes imperative. Aggression is not only a crime against the formal rules of international society; it is also, more importantly, an assault upon a people, a threat to their common life and even their physical survival. That is why particular acts of aggression, like the Iraqi invasion, *ought to be resisted*—not necessarily by military means but by some means. Though military means may be ruled out in practice in this or that case (because they are unlikely to be effective, or because they are frighteningly dangerous), they are never ruled out in principle. It is our abhorrence of aggression that is authoritative here, while the maxims of "last resort" and proportionality play only marginal and uncertain roles.

III

Just wars are limited wars; their conduct is governed by a set of rules designed to bar, so far as possible, the use of violence and coercion against noncombatant populations. The "government" of these rules, since it is not backed up by police power or authoritative courts, is to a large degree ineffective—but not entirely so. And even if the rules fail to shape the conduct of *this* war, they often succeed in shaping public judgments of conduct and so, perhaps, the training, commitment, and future conduct of soldiers. If war is an extension of politics, then military culture is an extension of political culture. Debate and criticism play an important, even if not a determinative, role in fixing the content of both these cultures.

Two forms of limit are crucial here, and both figured largely in the political defense, and then in the critique, of the Gulf War. The first has to do with the ends of war, the purposes for which it is fought. Just war theory, as it is usually understood, looks to the restoration of the status quo ante—the way things were, that is, before the aggression took place—with only one additional proviso: that the threat posed by the aggressor state in the weeks or months before its attack should not be included in this "restoration." Hence war aims legitimately reach to the destruction or to the defeat, demobilization, and (partial) disarming of the aggressor's armed forces. Except in extreme cases, like that of Nazi Germany, they don't legitimately reach to the transformation of the internal politics of the aggressor state or the replacement of its regime. For ends of this latter sort would require a prolonged occupation and massive coercion of civilians. More than this: they would require a usurpation of sovereignty, which is exactly what we condemn when we condemn aggression.

In the Iraqi case, the acceptance of this limit by the coalition opened the way, after the cease-fire, for a bloody civil war, whose civilian casualties may well exceed those of the war itself. The proportionality maxim would probably have dictated a quick and militarily inexpensive march on Baghdad. Limited wars are governed instead by the doctrine of nonintervention, which holds that changes of regime must be the work of the men and women who live under the regime—who also bear the costs of the change and the risks of failure. Nonintervention gives way to proportionality only in cases of massacre or of politically induced famine and epidemic, when the costs are unbearable. Then we are justified in acting or, more strongly, we ought to act (like the Vietnamese in Pol Pot's Cambodia, or the Tanzanians in Idi Amin's Uganda, or the Indians in what was then East Pakistan) without regard to the idea of sovereignty. It will seem hard to say, first, that we should not have intervened and made sure that the "right" side won the Iraqi civil war, and, second, that we should have intervened, much more quickly than we did, to rescue the victims of defeat. But the history of political, as distinct from humanitarian, interventions suggests that there are good reasons to make this distinction.

The same restorationist argument applies, more obviously, to the victim state, which is no more likely than the aggressor to be a bastion of sweetness and light (think of Haile Selassie's Ethiopian empire invaded by Italian fascists). Kuwait's regime was on balance superior to that of Iraq, but there are not many people in the world who would have rallied to its defense, even in print, had it been faced with a palace coup; a popular uprising would have been greeted almost everywhere with enthusiasm. And yet the purpose of the war was nothing more or less than the restoration of this regime, the semifeudal despotism of the al-Sabah family. What happened after that was (and is) the business of the Kuwaitis themselves, free from the coercion of foreign armies. They are not free, of course, from diplomatic pressure, or from human rights surveillance and agitation.

But the reversal of the aggression and the destruction of Iraqi military power were not the only goals of the coalition —or, at least, not the only goals of the United States in its role as organizer and leader of the coalition. Our government aimed also at a "new world order" in which its leading role, presumably, would be maintained. It was a common criticism of the war that the United States had "imperialist" motives: world order masked a desire for influence and power in the Gulf, for a strategic presence and control over the flow of oil. I assume that motives of this sort played an important part in American decision-making: even just wars have political as well as moral reasons—and will have, I expect, until the messianic age when justice will be done for its own sake. An absolutely singular motivation, a pure will, is a political illusion. The case is similar in domestic society, where we take it for granted that parties and movements fighting for civil rights or welfare reform do so because their members have certain values *and also* because they have certain ambitions—for power and office, say. Since they are not killing other people, this is easier to accept. But mixed motives are normal also in international politics, and they are morally troubling in wartime only if they make for the expansion or prolongation of the fighting beyond its justifiable limits or if they distort the conduct of the war.

It is entirely possible, then, to support a war within its justifiable limits and to oppose the added reasons this or that government has for fighting it. One could call for the defeat of Iraqi aggression and criticize at the same time the likely character of the "new world order." What is most important, however, is to insist that, new order or no, the war remain a limited war.

The second limit has to do with conduct—the everyday engagement of forces. The governing principle here is simply that every effort be made to protect civilian life from both direct attack and "collateral damage." How this principle fared in the Gulf War is best discussed in the context of the air campaign against Iraq, since war on the ground in desert environments tends to approach, effortlessly, as it were, the just war paradigm of a combat between combatants (there is still the question, though, of when and how such a combat should be brought to a halt). The coalition's military response to Iraq's invasion of Kuwait began with an air attack, and the war was fought almost exclusively with planes and missiles for some five weeks. The air war was described by American officers in press conferences and briefings in a language that combined technological jargon and just war theory. It was, we were told, a campaign directed with unprecedented precision solely at military targets. The bombs were "smart" and the pilots morally sensitive.

This effort to limit civilian casualties was embodied in clear-cut orders. Pilots were instructed to return to base with their bombs and missiles intact whenever they were unable to get a clear "fix" on their assigned targets. They were not to drop their bombs in the general vicinity of the targets; nor were they to aim freely at "targets of opportunity" (except in specified battle zones). In their bombing runs, they were to accept risks for themselves in order to reduce the risk of causing "collateral damage" to civilians. So we were told, and so, presumably, the pilots were told. The first studies of the bombing, after the war, suggest that those orders were often not followed—that bombs were commonly dropped from altitudes much too high for anything like confident aiming. But the policy, if it was the actual policy, was the right one. And it does appear that direct civilian casualties were kept fairly low: in this sense, at least, the air war was unprecedented.

The case is rather different if we look not at aiming policy but at the designated targets of that policy. The coalition decided (or the U.S. commanders decided) that the economic infrastructure of Iraqi society was—all of it—a legitimate military target: communication and transportation systems, electric power grids, government buildings of every sort, water pumping stations and purification plants. There was nothing unprecedented here; strategic bombing in World War II had a similar focus, though I don't believe that there was a systematic effort to deprive the German or Japanese people of clean water; perhaps this wasn't technically feasible in the 1940s. Selected infrastructural targets are easy enough to justify: bridges over which supplies are carried to the army in the field provide an obvious example. But power and water—water most clearly—are very much like food: they are necessary to the survival and everyday activity of soldiers, but they are equally necessary to everyone else. An attack here is an attack on civilian society. In this case, it is the military effects, if any, that are "collateral." The direct effect of the destruction of water purification plants, for example, was to impose upon civilians in urban areas (and Iraq is a highly urbanized society) the risks of disease in epidemic proportions.

Attacks of this sort suggest a war aim beyond the legitimate aim of "restoration plus"—the liberation of Kuwait and the defeat and reduction of Iraqi military power. The added, though never acknowledged, aim was presumably the overthrow of the Baathist regime, which was to be proven incapable not only of defending its foreign conquest but also of protecting its own people. But the aim is unjust and so is the means.

Indeed, even if we were justified in overthrowing the regime, we would have been barred from this cruel strategy of indirection—shattering Iraqi society so as to generate a desperate rebellion by its members. It would have been better to march on Baghdad. An exiled Iraqi dissident, writing just after the war, argued that since we had shattered Iraqi society, we were now bound to march on Baghdad and install a democratic government capable of organizing its reconstruction. I don't doubt that obligations of a significant sort can be incurred through wrongful actions in war. The difficulty with this particular example is the terrible presumption of the enterprise. Success was improbable anyway, and the likely human costs high.

There are other aspects of the conduct of the war that invite criticism and have received it—most importantly, the use of a frightening new weapon, the fuel air explosive, against Iraqi soldiers, and the air attacks, in the last days of the fighting, on what appears to have been not only an army in retreat but a routed and disorganized army in retreat. Just war theory as I understand it does not readily cover cases of this sort, where it is only soldiers who are under attack. Soldiers running away, unlike soldiers trying to surrender, are usually said to be legitimate targets: they may hope to fight another day. In this case, the Iraqi soldiers who succeeded in running away did fight another day— against rebellious fellow citizens. Here is yet another hard question for theorists of proportionality: should we have slaughtered retreating Iraqi soldiers in order to prevent the possible slaughter of Iraqi rebels? Standard just war arguments would probably come down against bombing the chaotic flight from Kuwait, precisely because the retreating army posed no threat *except* to its own people.

But this last point doesn't quite reach to our uneasiness with the spectacle of those last hours of the war, or to our relief when President Bush—too soon, some of his generals thought—called a halt to the killing. Justice is not the whole of morality. One may object to killing in war, even in just war, whenever it gets too easy. A "turkey shoot" is not a combat between combatants. When the world divides radically into those who bomb and those who are bombed, it becomes morally problematic, even if the bombing in this or that instance is justifiable.

It is still possible to defend some acts of war and unequivocally to condemn others. Nor can political and military leaders escape accountability by claiming that the acts that ought to be condemned were somehow entailed by the war itself and inevitable as soon as the fighting began. In fact, they required a distinct and independent decision by military strategists sitting around a table and arguing about what should be done—and then they required a further decision by politicians sitting around another table and arguing about the strategists' recommendations. It is easy enough to imagine the Gulf War without the attack on infrastructural targets. One might say that the point of just war theory is to make such imaginings obligatory.

IV

But if we are imagining versions of the world different from the one we have just experienced, why not imagine a world without war? This is not only or most importantly a pacifist or messianic dream—the lamb lying down with the lion. In one of its modes, just war theory would also abolish war by the (theoretically) simple method of calling unjust wars "crimes" and just wars "police actions." We have here a nice example of what the Chinese call "the rectification of names," but it presupposes in practice a thoroughgoing transformation of international society. Before there can be police actions, there must be police, and before there can be police, there must be a global authority capable of organizing and deploying police power. The United Nations does not have a capacity of that sort; nor can I think of any of its members who would be willing to assign to it a police force comparable to the coalition army assembled for the Gulf War. In principle, I suppose, such a force would not be burdened by mixed motives: the police enforce the law and suppress crime, and that is all they are supposed to do. In practice, however, police enforce the law selectively, and they have been used, much as armies have been used, to do many other things as well. A global authority, claiming a monopoly on the legitimate use of force, would be no less threatening than an imperial state.

What we have instead is an organization that authorizes its members to use force (the Korean War is the precedent, the Gulf War only the second case) but does not use force itself. Since any state can legitimately come to the aid of a victim of aggression, this authorization adds little to the moral, or even to the legal, argument. It plays, perhaps, a political and educational role: when the United Nations Security Council confirms the claim that a certain country, invaded by its neighbor, is indeed a victim of aggression, it makes rescue operations easier; and when it condemns the invasion, it gives voice to a general disapproval, which may have some deterrent effect. But confirmations and condemnations of this sort are uncertain at best. The United Nations machinery worked about as well as we can expect it to work on behalf of the Kuwaitis; it was of no use at all to the people of Tibet, say, among many others. And even when it works well, self-help, mutual aid, and collective security of an older kind are still necessary features of any struggle against aggression.

It would be a good thing, obviously, if every act of aggression was condemned by the United Nations and then resisted—politically and economically if possible, militarily if necessary—by a coalition of states. In fact, this will only happen sometimes, when enough states have reasons of their own to vote for condemnation and to join the coalition. But this is no reason to oppose the resistance—as if, having failed to rescue the Tibetans, we must now fail to rescue the Kuwaitis for the sake of moral consistency. Social critics have to argue for a consistent policy, which is to say that just war theory, with its definitions of aggression and self-defense and mutual aid, should be applied impartially across the society of states, to the critics' own state as well as to all the others. No doubt, such applications would be more attractive if it were also possible to set limits on their practical means and ends, to make sure that the wars we justify are fought justly. Here too states will prove unreliable agents, and that is why the argument about war and justice is still a political and moral necessity.

FROM LAST RESORT TO ENDGAME:

Morality, the Gulf War, and the Peace Process

GEORGE WEIGEL

Yes, it was.

In both intention and execution, the Gulf War was a justified war according to the classic canons of the just war tradition—the moral criteria by which thoughtful people in the West have wrestled with questions of force, power, violence, and the pursuit of peace since the days of St. Augustine. But before exploring precisely how the Gulf War met the moral tests set by the tradition, a few introductory words about the tradition itself are in order.

The just war tradition is about far more than military operations. It is in fact a theory of statecraft, and within that theory is embedded a crucial concept of the peace that is possible—and thus morally obligatory to pursue—in this kind of world. While its opponents sometimes charge that the tradition is fatally compromised from the outset—"doing ethics for Caesar," as one prominent pacifist theologian has described the work of his nonpacifist colleagues—the

19

tradition at its best has worked to forge moral, political, and strategic links between the limited use of armed force and the pursuit of peace with freedom, justice, security, and order.

This linkage rests on a central claim of the just war tradition: namely, that "morality" and "politics" do not exist in hermetically sealed compartments of life. Rather, the tradition insists that there is one indivisible human universe of thought and action, a universe that is, at one and the same time, inescapably moral and inescapably political. Political and military decisions are not, in this tradition, simply matters of *is;* they inevitably involve questions of *ought,* too.

Critics also charge that the tradition is too often ambiguous, and that it rarely offers clear-cut "answers" to statesmen and military leaders. But this criticism rests on a misunderstanding of the nature of moral reasoning in the just war tradition. The just war tradition is not a kind of intellectual cookie cutter, and its practitioners should not be understood as bakers on an assembly line. Or, to vary the imagery, moral reasoning within the just war tradition is far more like a skilled musical conductor interpreting a symphonic score than it is like an engineer reading a blueprint. The conductor has notes and other instructions on his score. But the beauty (or dissonance) of the music he or she makes is a function, not simply of the notes, but of the application of the conductor's imagination, intelligence, and discipline. And so it is with the notes—the norms—of the just war tradition.

The Just War Tradition and the Gulf War

The just war tradition includes two clusters of moral criteria: the six criteria of the *jus ad bellum* ("war-decision law," the rules that determine when the resort to armed force is mor-

20

ally justified), and the two criteria of the *jus in bello* ("war-conduct law," the rules that govern the justifiable use of armed force in combat). All eight of the just war criteria were vigorously debated before, during, and after the Gulf War. A review of how U.S. policy satisfied all eight of these moral standards can help frame the debate over the use of armed force in the future.

War-Decision Law
1. *Just Cause.* Iraq's invasion and attempted annexation of Kuwait violated the most fundamental norms of international public life. We also know, and in even more grisly detail than was available through the Amnesty International report in late 1990, that Iraq conducted a brutal campaign of torture and terror within occupied Kuwait—a campaign that, even by the debased standards of the neighborhood, was a monstrous evil. Moreover, Iraq's relentless quest for weapons of mass destruction, and for the means to deliver them far beyond its borders, was a grave threat to even a minimum of peace and security in the Middle East, and beyond. (That Iraq would not have hesitated to use such weapons as instruments of political terror was graphically illustrated by the Scud attacks on Tel Aviv on the second day of the allied air campaign.) These factors indisputably constituted a "just cause" for military intervention—as, I would argue, did Iraq's threat to control some 40 percent of the world's proven oil reserves, a threat that, if executed, would have massively disrupted the world economy (striking hardest at the poorest countries) while concurrently fueling the further expansion of Iraq's military machine and its pursuit of nuclear weapons.

2. *Right Intention.* Wars for revenge, wars to satisfy bloodlust or imperial ambitions, are not justifiable under the tradition's criterion of "right intention." The Gulf War, though, was a different kind of war. It was not a war aimed

21

at the destruction of Iraq; as the President insisted from the beginning, our enemy was not the people of Iraq, but the Saddam Hussein regime. The United States engaged Iraq militarily in pursuit of three political-military goals: to reverse a great evil—the occupation, attempted annexation, and rape of Kuwait; to check the growth of Iraq's offensive military capability, and particularly its pursuit of weapons of mass destruction; and to establish some basic ground rules for the conduct of international political and economic affairs in the post–Cold War world. These were honorable intentions. They were, according to the tradition, "right intentions."

3. *Competent Authority.* The use of armed force by the United States was authorized by a democratically elected President and supported by a democratically elected Congress. Congress's decision to support the President followed an open and vigorous debate that directly engaged the moral issues involved in the Gulf crisis. The use of armed force by the coalition led by the United States was authorized by a resolution of the Security Council of the United Nations. At every significant decision point between August 2, 1990, and February 28, 1991, the United States engaged in extensive consultations with its principal allies, including major Arab states. In short, the Gulf War was authorized, not just once, but in a continuing process of international agreement, by all the relevant "competent authorities."

4. *Reasonable Chance of Success.* The just war tradition has no room within it for kamikaze military actions, or even for romantic acts of soldierly bravado. Precisely because it tries to order the use of force to the pursuit of peace, and precisely because it sets moral boundaries around the use of force, the tradition requires us to judge, before we engage militarily, that there is a "reasonable chance" that our actions will be militarily successful.

There were extensive arguments about the possibilities

for military success before January 16, 1991, and just before the ground war began on February 24. Americans argued about the relative merits of an extended air campaign. We argued at length, and passionately, about the possible dangers of a ground war. At every point along this line, the President and his advisers gathered information and sought counsel in a deliberate and careful way. Their confidence in our strategists and theater commanders, and their judgments about the possibilities of our success—in November 1990, when our ground forces in Saudi Arabia were significantly enhanced; in early January 1991, just before the air campaign began; and in February 1991, before the ground war—were vindicated by subsequent events.

5. *Proportionality of Ends.* Would the good that might be achieved by driving Iraq from Kuwait outweigh the evil that would be caused by allowing Iraq's aggression to stand? We cannot know for sure, even now, what the full ramifications of our military victory will be for the politics and economics of the Middle East, and indeed of the world. Which is to say, we cannot measure the amplitude of the good that has been achieved to date. That is in the nature of things.

But we could know with clarity, even in the fall of 1990, that a failure to check Iraqi aggression would have serious consequences for the region and the world. An already unstable and volatile area would become even more of a powder keg. Kuwaiti society (we could expect even then) would be virtually dismantled, and torture would be widespread. An unscrupulous dictator, armed to the teeth and aggressively seeking even more destructive capability, would have positioned himself as the strongman of the Arab world. A great evil had been committed already, and more evils were surely to follow. Ejecting Iraq from Kuwait, and checking Saddam Hussein's drive for regional hegemony, were morally justified ends according to the "war-decision" criterion of proportionality.

23

6. *Last Resort.* Here, of course, is where much of the congressional debate was focused in early January 1991. Had economic sanctions been given enough time? Had all diplomatic means of resolving the conflict been tried?

In the just war tradition, "last resort" is not an arithmetic concept. One can always imagine "one more" nonmilitary tactic that could be tried, one more negotiating effort that could be launched, one more conference that could be called—in a sequence that is, by definition, infinite in duration. No, what the tradition means by "last resort" is that reasonable people can reasonably conclude that all reasonable efforts at a nonmilitary solution have been tried, have failed, and in all probability will continue to fail.

The judgment made in January 1991 that U.S. military action against Iraq satisfied the criterion of "last resort" was a reasonable and prudent judgment at the time, as subsequent events have confirmed. Economic sanctions are, on occasion, a useful instrument of international policy. But there was little evidence prior to January 16, 1991, that economic sanctions would make a serious dent in Saddam Hussein's regime and its capabilities. The regime was, after all, a tightly organized and ruthlessly controlled police state, in which military and governmental personnel would be the last to feel the "bite" of economic sanctions. The Iraqi dictator's conduct of the war—his persistent violations of the laws of war, his disregard for civilian casualties, his commitment to an attrition strategy that cost his armed forces dearly—reinforced that view, as indeed his draconian conduct of the affairs of his country for a dozen years should have reinforced it in the debate prior to January 16. Claims from certain "conflict resolution specialists," who asserted that Saddam's attempted incorporation of Kuwait into Iraq could have been reversed by more active "win-win" diplomacy, simply put one in mind of Orwell's famous observation, that some propositions are so preposterous that only intellectuals could possibly believe them.

The course of the war after January 16, 1991, and the details of what had happened in Kuwait since August 2, 1990, raise even more questions about the "give sanctions a chance" school of thought. We know, now, that thousands of Kuwaitis were killed, tortured, raped, or otherwise brutalized while we were "giving sanctions a chance," and there is every reason to think that the pillage of Kuwait would have continued unabated had the "sanctions only" policy prevailed in January. Moreover, Iraq used the time between August 1990 and January 1991 to dig itself in along the Saudi-Kuwaiti border. The military contest was thus bloodier than it otherwise might have been (and precisely for the Iraqi conscripts who manned those border bunkers) because we gave sanctions five and a half months to "work."

Finally, there is the matter of Saddam Hussein himself. No one who had made even a cursory study of this man's career could reasonably have assumed that he would be swayed by the voice of reason, or by economic hardships imposed on the people of his country. Unhappily, it took the invasion of Kuwait to drive this point home to the Department of State and its Bureau of Near Eastern Affairs. But past misperceptions and errors do not constitute an argument against action once the fog of confusion and misapprehension has lifted. Listening to some of the critics of the Gulf War, one would have thought that the United States should have done penance for the past sins of the Near Eastern Bureau by leaving Saddam Hussein in possession of Kuwait. But that is, prima facie, a morally absurd position.

The use of armed force in the Gulf by the United States and its coalition allies fully satisfied the just war criterion of "last resort." Arguments to the contrary, today, make little sense indeed.

War-Conduct Law

1. *Proportionality of Means.* The just war tradition tries to build moral boundaries against the excessive use of military force, even in cases when the resort to arms is deemed morally justifiable. "Proportionality" in the tradition's war-conduct law requires that we use no more military force than is necessary in order to achieve morally legitimate political and military objectives.

"Proportionality of means" has been debated continuously in the aftermath of the Gulf War. Indeed, judging from the press calls I was getting some twenty-four hours into the ground war, the argument began while the war was still under way, given the large numbers of Iraqi casualties along the Saudi-Kuwaiti border, and the U.S. and coalition attacks on retreating Iraqi forces.

Yet even in the immediate aftermath of the war, with casualty figures still unclear, there were a number of points that could be made in defense of the proposition that the United States and its coalition partners had indeed met the war-conduct criterion of proportionality in both the air and ground campaigns.

In the first instance, it was clear from the outset that the coalition was conducting a war not against the Iraqi nation, but against its political-military leadership, its regime infrastructure, and its capacity to mount offensive military actions in the immediate future. This was not, to repeat, a war against the people of Iraq—although it is surely the case that the people of Iraq suffered greatly during this war, and after it. The power grid that provided electrical capacity to Saddam's regime and military infrastructure also helped light Iraqi homes and hospitals. And that, tragically, is one of the things that wars do: they cause suffering beyond the battlefield, particularly when one of the combatants has organized his country such that attacks on military targets will almost inevitably have aftereffects on civilians. But the relevant moral question is whether that suffering outside the theater of combat was directly intended (as was the case with Saddam Hussein's Scud attacks on Tel Aviv, Haifa, and Riyadh), or whether it was the result of legitimate military actions.

Then there is the question of Iraqi military casualties. Iraq suffered a very large number of combat deaths. Were those numbers "disproportionate"?

There were many Iraqi troops killed in the air campaign against the fortifications along the Saudi-Kuwaiti border. But what was the alternative to an air campaign against those fortifications? A frontal assault with ground forces? That would certainly have resulted in even larger casualty figures on both sides.

There were many Iraqi troops killed during the mother of all retreats, in the third and fourth days of the ground war. Were U.S. and coalition forces simply engaged in a "turkey shoot" on the road out of Kuwait, as some put it? No, they were not. By the second day of the ground war, it was clear that surrender was an option for Iraqis who understood that there was no escape from the overwhelming military superiority of the allies. At least fifty thousand and perhaps eighty thousand, Iraqis had surrendered (some of them to Italian TV crews!) by the time questions began to be raised about U.S. and coalition attacks on retreating Iraqi forces. Those in retreat had an alternative to being attacked: they could surrender. Moreover, had Iraq managed to salvage a considerable remnant of its armor from the war, we would have been faced with the possibility of an extended war, or a war that re-erupted after weeks of stalling in "negotiations."

The death of tens of thousands of Iraqi soldiers is a human tragedy. It is not a tragedy that would have been mitigated in the slightest by higher coalition casualty figures. Those Iraqi deaths lie squarely on the moral account of Saddam Hussein, who put his forces in harm's way to satisfy his own megalomaniacal ambitions. The argument will surely continue, but my judgment is that the United States and its coalition allies met the criterion of "proportionality of means" in their conduct of the war.

2. *Discrimination.* This is the just war criterion with which all reflective people are familiar: in a justified war, military operations must rigorously discriminate between combatants and noncombatants.

The early days of the air war demonstrated not merely that coalition forces intended to observe the just war principle of discrimination, but that they had weapons capable of achieving precisely that moral aim. The story told by the BBC's John Simpson about his experiences in Baghdad in the first days of the air war is a familiar one by now, but it bears repeating all the same: "When the air force general said the Al Rasheed Hotel was a turning place for cruise missiles, he meant it literally: one flew across the front of the hotel, turned at the corner, and flew across the back of it before striking its target just opposite."

Throughout the war, U.S. pilots operated under strict rules of target recognition, and by all accounts they seem to have tried to obey them scrupulously, to the point of bringing back unexpended ordnance when targets were not clearly identifiable. Their task was not simplified by the tactics of Saddam Hussein: using command-and-control centers as civilian shelters; parking combat aircraft near religious and archaeological sites; using civilian convoys as camouflage for mobile Scud launchers.

And yet, despite the coalition's precautions, there were civilian casualties. That, too, is unavoidable in war. But were these intentional casualties? No. Did the United States and its coalition partners use air power indiscriminately, as had been common practice in World War II? No. Did modern weapons make war inherently more indiscriminate? No. (In fact, the opposite is more likely true.) Iraqi civilian casu-

alties are a cause for sorrow. They are not a cause for guilt
—except on the part of Saddam Hussein and those of his
clique who maintained him (and themselves) in power.

The Endgame

The Gulf War thus satisfied the eight classic criteria of the
just war tradition, and in a manner that is quite arguably
unprecedented in modern warfare. That judgment, I believe, remains true despite two inescapable, and morally
troubling, facts: that the war ended rather sloppily, with
Saddam Hussein still in power, and that Saddam visited
great suffering on the Shiites of southern Iraq and the Kurds
in the north in the months after the U.S.-Iraqi cease-fire.
Indeed, contrary to the claims made in the postwar period
by some who had opposed the war from the outset—claims
to the effect that the postwar sufferings of the Shiites and
Kurds demonstrated that the war was never justifiable—the
more morally and politically plausible judgment is that the
United States erred by stopping the war too soon: perhaps
by as little as two or three days too soon. Five points about
the war's endgame may be made briefly:

1. It seemed to me, after a trip to the Middle East in late
August and early September of 1990, that no morally and
politically satisfactory resolution of the Gulf crisis was possible so long as Saddam Hussein remained in power in Baghdad.

According to some reliable reports, U.S. strategy was oriented in a similar direction, and the decision to stop the
ground war on February 28 may well have been influenced
in part by the judgment that the Baath Party and the remains of the Iraqi military would depose Saddam Hussein in
short order.

If that in fact was one of the assumptions shaping the

policy decision to halt offensive operations in Iraq, it was a serious tactical misjudgment. Absent any coalition military pressure, Saddam Hussein clung to power and conducted an extraordinary campaign of internal repression that seems to have secured his regime's power in Iraq. And while Saddam's conventional military power has been checked (at least in the near term), his continuing quest for nuclear, chemical, and biological weapons of mass destruction is a cause for great concern.

2. The decision to stop the ground war when we did was undoubtedly the result of many factors and vectors of influence. But on the basis of conversations I had subsequently with some of those involved, at both the White House and the Pentagon, I am convinced that the decision to stop on February 28 was driven, in part, by a moral concern: namely, that the United States and its allies were bumping up against the boundaries of proportionality in our attack on the retreating Iraqi troops coming out of Kuwait. The moral tragedy of that moral concern is that, in an effort to stop the killing, we brought about circumstances in which far more innocents were in fact slain by the remnants of Saddam Hussein's military and his internal security apparatus. Surely there were options available to us between continuing an unremitting attack on retreating Iraqi forces and unilaterally halting the ground war.

3. The most morally dubious part of U.S. policy in the immediate postwar period was to permit Saddam Hussein to use helicopters and fixed-wing aircraft in crushing the Kurdish rebellion in the north and the Shiite rebellion in the south—at a time when we had uncontested air superiority throughout Iraq, and after we had publicly encouraged the rebellions that Saddam Hussein was crushing. By encouraging these rebellions, the United States assumed a measure of responsibility, limited but real, to provide reasonable assistance to those who acted on the (not unreasonable) as-

sumption that they would be supported by the United States. Failure to do so was morally offensive, and strategically inept.

4. Moreover, there *were* alternatives for the United States other than getting militarily embroiled in an Iraqi civil war, or doing essentially nothing.

We could have kept Saddam Hussein's forces out of the air.

We could have declared ourselves the protectors of the Shiite holy places in southern Iraq, and we could have taken out any Iraqi military forces that were likely to have done damage to those shrines (as indeed we were urged to do by an Iraqi Shiite ayatollah).

We could have created safe havens—through the interposition of coalition forces, to be followed by United Nations forces—for the Kurds and Shiites.

We could have worked with the Turks and with the Iraqi opposition toward the creation of a more loosely federated Iraq, with significant regional autonomy for the Kurds and the Shiites. This would doubtless have involved serious arm twisting with the Saudis. But if we could not bring ourselves to do this in March 1991—when we had, without exaggeration, just saved the Saudi regime from extinction—then it is hard to imagine the circumstances when we would exert serious leverage.

5. U.S. policy between August 2, 1990, and February 28, 1991, was a success precisely because it linked moral, political, strategic, and military considerations together. The fracturing of *that* intellectual coalition, so to speak, was a serious error. Subsequent reports have indicated that the Administration's decisions in March 1991 were guided in considerable part by what officials understood to be the principles of realpolitik. But, all claims to the contrary notwithstanding, realpolitik is not an escape from moral reasoning; it is a debased form of moral reasoning. Doing the

right thing "worked" from August 2, 1990, through February 28, 1991: doing the right thing made for a potent politics and strategy on behalf of peace with a measure of security, order, freedom, and justice. There was no reason, after February 28, 1991, to think that America had to march to a different moral (or amoral) drummer.

Winning the Peace

The failures of Administration policy in the endgame of the Gulf War do not, in and of themselves, invalidate the judgment that the war itself was justified, in intention or execution. But those errors did make it far more difficult to win the peace.

And that should be of special concern to those who thought about the Gulf War from within the just war tradition. Why? Because the tradition is more than a moral calculus for determining when the resort to armed force is morally justified and how that armed force is to be used in a justified war. For, in addition to the classic criteria of the *jus ad bellum* and the *jus in bello,* the just war tradition also contains what I have called an *jus ad pacem:* a theory of statecraft, in which is embedded an important concept of peace.

The theory of statecraft implicit in the just war tradition requires that the use of proportionate and discriminate armed force be ordered to the pursuit of peace in all of its component parts: freedom, justice, security, and order. The peace envisioned by the tradition is not the utopian peace of a world without conflict, but the peace of a world in which law and politics—rightly ordered legal and political institutions—are the normal means of prosecuting and resolving conflict. This is, I take it, at least part of what President Bush means by a "new world order." But since the just war tradition, in its understanding of the peace that is possible in this world, dates back to St. Augustine in the fifth century, the "new world order" may be not so new after all. Nor need it be tethered to a Wilsonian optimism and naiveté about the nature of politics among nations. The "new world order" can and should be built on the far more secure foundations of Augustinian realism—amplified by a little of that optimism about human possibilities that characterized the political thought of St. Thomas Aquinas, the first Whig.

But not too much optimism. The difficulties of winning the peace in the wake of successfully ejecting Iraq from Kuwait are a useful, if sobering, reminder of the intractable character of many dimensions of the conflict between Israel and its Arab neighbors. "Intractability" is not a category with which Americans are very comfortable; we are fixers and problem solvers, and it is difficult for us to enter into the mental universe of people who may regard long-standing political conflicts not as problems to be solved, but as struggles to be won—and won in a winner-take-all fashion.

In retrospect, and even in light of the prospect of a new round of Mideast negotiations that may include direct, bilateral talks between Israel and Arab states, it seems clear (as it always does in retrospect, alas) that too many hopes were invested in the Gulf War as a logjam-breaking event that would so change the correlation of forces in the Middle East that a grand settlement of the region's post-1948 conflicts would become possible. That, unhappily, has not happened.

The sloppy endgame of the Gulf War is one reason why: Saddam Hussein, for as long as he remains in power, will be viewed by many Arabs as the real victor in the war, the man who faced down the United States, the United Kingdom, France, and numerous other countries. The corrosive impact of this perception on the leverage that the United States enjoys in the region can be imagined.

Failures of American postwar policy are another reason

why things seem to have shifted very little, in the politics of the Middle East, from the status quo ante–August 2, 1990. The pusillanimity—there is, unfortunately, no other word for it—that the United States displayed vis-à-vis the governments of Saudi Arabia and Kuwait in the months immediately following the war suggests not only an imbalance in the Administration's perceptions of the obstacles to peace in the region, but, perhaps even more disturbingly, a singular unwillingness to exert pressure (or, less boldly, to forcefully press a case) on our recent Arab allies in terms of new approaches to the continuing war against Israel. Nor should we soon forget the intransigence of both the Saudi and Kuwaiti governments on the question of peace with Israel once their immediate security concerns had been assuaged.

So it is perhaps time to lower our expectations. No grand settlement seems possible now. (Whether it might have been possible had we pursued the war until Saddam was toppled and a different—possibly federal, and certainly militarily nonthreatening—Iraq emerged from the rubble of defeat is a question to which we shall quite probably never have an answer.) But some important steps toward winning the peace over time could be taken—if the United States, in its pursuit of the "peace process," takes the concept of worldly and political "peace" embedded in the just war tradition as seriously as it took the tradition's war-decision rules and war-conduct rules.

Peace-for-Peace
The first and most crucial of these steps might be called "peace-for-peace."

The Gulf War—the fact that it happened, and the dynamics of the coalition politics by which it was fought—should have put to rest the notion that the "Palestinian problem" is the cause of all the other woes of the Middle East. That was never the case, as the Gulf War amply demonstrated.

34

Rather, the two central problems that must be addressed if there is to be a minimum of the peace of order in the Middle East are the continuing Arab war against Israel and the instability of Arab political regimes.

With the honorable exception of Egypt, virtually the entire Arab world has been in a formal state of war with Israel since 1948—forty-four years. Until that fact is changed, there is no path to peace open in the region. The state of war against Israel must end.

As noted earlier, the United States had a considerable amount of leverage with key Arab states in the wake of the Gulf War. With Arab partners, we had successfully fought a coalition war against an aggressive Arab state, and had done so without mass turmoil on the "Arab street." Pan-Arabism seemed dead, or at least dying. March 1991, then, was the golden moment to suggest to our coalition partners, quietly but firmly, that the time had come to offer peace-for-peace: to declare the forty-three-year-old war with Israel to be at an end, and to recognize (through an exchange of diplomatic missions and the end of the Arab economic boycott) the permanent reality of the fact of Israel in the Middle East, without foreclosing any future arguments about the final disposition of borders in the region. That the Administration did not seize this opportunity is the diplomatic corollary to its strategic and tactical errors in the war's endgame. But there is no reason why the concept of peace-for-peace cannot be injected by the United States into the "peace process" at any time of our choosing.

Land-for-peace is a nonstarter until the forty-four-year-old war ends. That conclusion should have suggested itself to anyone familiar with the post-1948 history of the region, as well as to anyone who had thought carefully about the dynamics of peacemaking that Anwar Sadat let loose by his visit to Jerusalem: land-for-peace (in Sadat's case, the Sinai) followed peace-for-peace (Sadat's declaration in Jerusalem that he was determined to end Egypt's war with Israel). The analogy is, like all analogies, imperfect: the Golan Heights and the West Bank are not the Sinai, strategically or psychologically. But the fact remains that the one great break in the otherwise unremitting armed conflict between Israel and the Arab states came when the establishment of peace-for-peace preceded negotiations over land-for-peace. In the aftermath of the war, it is surely past time for the United States to take a principled position to this effect: peace-for-peace is where the path to peace begins.

Confidence-building Measures
Winning the peace over the long haul will also involve short- and medium-term confidence-building measures, to borrow a term from the world of nuclear arms control. Some possibilities on this front were bruited in the months immediately following the war: a regional ban on ballistic missiles; a Middle East nuclear weapons–free zone; restrictions on the importation of further military hardware into the region. These suggestions are surely worth pursuing, but it would also seem useful—from the point of view of the just war tradition and its concept of statecraft—to focus some energy on building elements of the infrastructure of the peace of order in and among the nations of the Middle East.

Think, for example, of the development of cooperative economic enterprises in which peoples now divided by tribe, race, or religion can work together in creating new wealth and bettering their own personal economic circumstances. It is an admittedly rough rule of thumb, but it seems to have proven itself over time: people engaged in making money together—or in making money from each other—are far less likely to be found cutting each other's throats at the first opportunity. A joint attack on the problem of water resources in the Jordan Valley by Israelis, Lebanese, Jordanians, and now-stateless Palestinians might provide a model for similar cooperative enterprises over time.

Then there is the question of democratization in the region. Ever since the Gulf War began with Saddam Hussein's invasion of Kuwait on August 2, 1990, there has been considerable talk about the "democracy option" as the way to peace in the Middle East. Here, too, a measure of idealism without illusions (or, if you prefer, realism without cynicism) is in order.

It is certainly true that, under modern conditions—an educated populace, mass communications, rising economic expectations, pluralism—authoritarian regimes are inherently unstable. Why? Because they lack the legitimacy that comes, in the world today, from popular consent.

It is also true that Arab culture has shown itself generally resistant to the democratic idea and to democratic processes. This will not change overnight, although in fact there are some signs of progress visible even now.

Given these two realities, and the tension between them, prudent policy aimed at confidence building among the many warring parties in the Middle East (and it should always be remembered that the axis of conflict in the region does not merely run along the Israeli-Arab fault line) would seem to require us to encourage the creation of the building blocks of democratic political *culture* throughout the Arab Middle East: a freer press; consultative assemblies; legally protected opposition political parties; trade unions; business associations; voluntary associations, including human rights groups. I would even be prepared to suggest to our coalition partners that something has to be done about the dire state of religious freedom in the Arab Middle East.

Concurrently, American and other Western friends of Israel must press that beleaguered democracy to undertake long-overdue reforms in its own democratic process, particularly in terms of its electoral system and the low threshold level of votes required for a seat in the Knesset. Democratization in the Arab world will be difficult enough, given the historical and cultural factors in play. It will be made even more difficult if the region's only democracy remains semiparalyzed in its politics because of the inordinate influence of fringe elements whose programs are magnified far beyond their level of public support by an irrationally rationalistic system of proportional representation.

The Palestinian Imbroglio

The concept of peace-for-peace, and the strategy of using confidence-building measures on both the hardware (or military) and "software" (or political) sides of the Middle East equation, should also be applied to the Palestinian issue.

Thanks in large measure to the Palestinians themselves, the "Palestinian problem" got much worse during the Gulf War. It was bad enough when Yasir Arafat, from whom little else should have been expected, embraced Saddam Hussein immediately after the invasion of Kuwait. But even the Israeli peace camp was shaken to its foundations by the sight of Palestinians cheering Scud missiles—the same Palestinians who demanded gas masks while calling on Saddam Hussein to launch chemical warfare against Israel. The Palestinian embrace of Saddam Hussein is said to have been an act of "desperation"; but that was said of the Palestinian embrace of the Soviet Union during the Cold War, as it was said of the Palestinian embrace of Hitler during World War II. At some point, and perhaps that point has now been reached, psychobabble wears thin, and reality finally obtrudes.

That the Palestine Liberation Organization has been dramatically discredited (and, perhaps more importantly, defunded) by its embrace of Saddam Hussein is in fact good news, for it opens up the possibility that a new Palestinian leadership will emerge. Were that to happen, as it perhaps might through open and carefully scrutinized elections in the Occupied Territories, the new Palestinian leadership should understand that the fulfillment of its national aspirations requires it to commit itself to four steps, which have already been discussed:

It must commit itself to peace-for-peace, recognizing without cavil the permanence of Israel in the region.

It must participate openly in regional economic development projects.

It must assist in the process of regional security stabilization, by putting an end to Palestinian terrorism once and for all, and by committing itself to the pursuit of a disarmed Palestinian homeland.

And it must commit itself to democratization, which means the emergence of multiple Palestinian political parties and a free Palestinian press.

A Living Tradition

The debate over possible U.S. military intervention in the war launched by Saddam Hussein on August 2, 1990, was loud, raucous, sharp, occasionally sloppy, sometimes startlingly insightful: in a word, democratic. It was also, arguably, unprecedented in the contemporary world. Could one imagine a similar debate in France prior to one of the Fifth Republic's quondam African adventures? Or in Britain before the Falklands War? Viewed from one angle, then, the moral*ism* that had debased the Vietnam argument in the United States seems to have been replaced by a capacity for genuinely public *moral argument* on large issues of the national interest and the national purpose.

Nor was it an accident that the categories in which Americans from across the socioeconomic spectrum debated the

Gulf issue were the classic categories of the just war tradition. Cab drivers, talk show hosts, barbers, columnists, and politicians were all working the issue in remarkably similar terms: Who was the "competent authority" in this case? What constituted a "last resort"? Did we have a "reasonable chance of success"? But this really shouldn't have been a surprise. Americans instinctively argued in these categories because the just war tradition reflects those moral intuitions that natural law theorists have long believed are built into human beings, and because the just war tradition is a rational tradition of moral discourse with the ability to provide a grammar for public moral argument in a pluralistic society.

It was a curiosity of the debate that the country's formal religious leadership, which might have been expected to be the bearer of this venerable tradition of moral reasoning, contributed so little to the argument. The National Council of Churches, on the basis of its record in the Gulf War, is now functionally pacifist, and its judgments on international politics reflect in pristine form that sixties sensibility which blames America first, early, and often. The National Conference of Catholic Bishops formally entered the Gulf debate in November 1990 and helped deepen the just war argument through letters to President Bush and Secretary Baker and through congressional testimony. But, as had been the case in the 1980s debates on nuclear weapons and Central America, the bishops' analysis was heavily influenced by a reading of the international political realities that was, to be charitable, less than persuasive. On the other hand, the Gulf War debate became the occasion for a serious wrestling with the just war tradition by many evangelical Protestants whose use of the tradition was not previously overdeveloped.

That the just war tradition—its moral logic and its historic applications—is more rigorously studied at West Point and

Annapolis than in liberal Protestant and Roman Catholic seminaries may seem, to some, a curiosity, just as it may appear odd that op-ed columnists and members of Congress sometimes show a more intimate familiarity with the criteria of the tradition than do archbishops and other church executives. One may hope that the Gulf War debate will encourage a rediscovery of the riches of this tradition of moral reasoning among church leaders across the country.

Still, the positive lesson for the moment is that the just war tradition is a living tradition in American public life. The tradition does not, and cannot, guarantee wise foreign policy in and of itself. But it can help ensure, as it did in the Gulf War, that the ends and means of American power are debated against an intellectual horizon in which it is understood that political and military questions are inescapably moral questions, too.

JUST WAR
AS POLITICS:

What the Gulf War Told Us About Contemporary American Life

JEAN BETHKE ELSHTAIN

Just war is not just about war. It is a way of thinking that refuses to separate politics from ethics. Unlike the competing doctrine of realism, or realpolitik, just war argument insists one cannot sever public and private moralities altogether; that one must not open up a sharp divide between "domestic" and "international" politics. Realism and just war theory embrace contrasting presumptions about the human condition. For the realist, struggle is endemic to that condition and force can neither be evaded nor avoided; the point, rather, is to use force cleverly, to one's own strategic advantage. For the just war thinker, viewing humanity and history through the hermeneutic of original sin, war and the use of force may be a terrible necessity but violence is always a tragedy rather than the definitive sign of humanity's essence. Human motives and actions are mixed. It follows that war, when it occurs, is as likely to be an expression of justifiable outrage at injustice as an ineluctable bursting forth of our innate brutishness. Might never makes right, argues the just war thinker, but might may sometimes, on balance, serve right.

The realpolitiker insists that the rules which govern "private" moral conduct are inapplicable to the world of "men and states." Just war politics insists that, although it would be utopian to presume that relations between states can be governed by the promises and caretaking apposite in our dealings with family and friends, this does not mean a war of all against all must kick in once one leaves the hearth or the immediate neighborhood. The realist is governed by prudential calculations, the just war thinker by a complex amalgam of normative principles and pragmatic evaluations.[1]

As a theory of war fighting and resort to war, just war thinking is a cluster of injunctions: what it is permissible to do; what it is not permissible to do. For example, a war must be the last resort; a war must be openly and legally declared; a war must be a response to a specific instance of unjust aggression; the means deployed in fighting a war must be proportionate to ends; a war must be waged in such a way as to distinguish combatants from noncombatants. Whether in evaluating a resort to arms or in determining the bases and nature of political order more generally, the just war thinker holds certain truths to be self-evident. One is a belief in the existence of universal moral dispositions leading men and women everywhere to establish norms and rules for the just and unjust taking of life. A second is an insistence on the need for moral judgments, for being able to figure out who in fact in the situation at hand is behaving in a more or less

1. Realism comes in many varieties. My use of "the realist" as a contrast to "the just war thinker" no doubt oversimplifies realism for analytic and polemical purposes. A realist moralist—George Kennan comes to mind—may make common cause with the just war thinker in seeking limits to violence and to the utopianism of a resort to force as a way to cure our ills and rid us of our torments. Kennan writes of the moral and spiritual qualities of "man himself." This is a far cry from the brutality of the Athenian generals in the Melian dialogue or the almost casual cruelty Machiavelli endorses in the name of *virtù*.

just or unjust manner; who is more the victimizer and who the victim. As well, just war insists on the power of moral appeals and arguments, repudiating realist cynicism in this matter. For the realist, moral appeals are always so much icing on the cake of strategic considerations. For the just war thinker, moral appeals are the heart of the matter—not the only matter but the place from which one starts.

Just war thinkers insist that they are not propounding immutable rules so much as clarifying the circumstances that should—and actually, if imperfectly, do—justify a state in going to war *(jus ad bellum),* and what is and is not allowable in fighting the wars to which a state has committed itself *(jus in bello).* Alas, much just war argumentation is often enormously abstract, featuring recondite discussions about double effect, collateral damage, and so on. Whatever importance this mode of argumentation may have for moral theologians and ethicists of a formal sort, it fails to make contact with those genuine civic possibilities and concerns which form the focus of this essay. For we human beings, in our ordinary thoughts and actions, don't think in and through categories of complex systematicity. We reason in terms of horror, brutality, and bravery when we think of war. These powerful recognitions frame our sense of what is just or unjust. And what we bring to bear in war's terrible circumstances will be shaped by whether what is foremost in our minds at a given moment is the suffering of a starving child, her food sources cut off by an embargo or economic sanctions, or a threat to the autonomy of a nation-state, not so much as a legalistic entity but as a people and a way of life.

There are those who argue that our moral squeamishness must be laid to rest in times of war; the image of the starving child put out of sight and out of mind. This is cruel, yes, they say, but we live in a cruel and dangerous world and we must think in terms of the Big Picture, the system of sovereign states and a balance of forces. For if we do not think in this way, if we are naive about the world's ways, many more children will suffer over the long run as smaller nations are gobbled up by huge empires and tyrants run amok. Just war insists that we can hold within a single frame a concern with peoples in a collective sense and a commitment to the individual. Clearly, just war thinking requires much of us. It demands deep reflection on what our governments are up to. It presupposes a "self" or citizen of a certain kind, one attuned to moral reasoning and capable of it; one strong enough to resist the lure of the seductive enthusiasms of violence; one laced through with a sense of responsibility and accountability; in other words, a morally formed civic character.

What just war thinking as a civic philosophy has to offer is this: what is an expectation requiring little justification for the realist—war, violence, resort to force—requires explanation and justification for the just war thinker. An additional strength of just war thinking is that it pictures the individual within a framework of overlapping communities, commitments, and loyalties: families, civil society, the state. Just war is an account of politics that, as I indicated at the outset, places politics within an ethically shaped framework and commits its adherents—by definition, all citizens who share some sense, however loosely defined, of just and unjust, fair and unfair—to debates of a particular kind whenever and wherever a resort to force is contemplated.

It is important to see just war thinking in its full elaboration as a theory of international and domestic politics, for this gives us leverage we might otherwise lack to evaluate the way the inner determination of states shapes the dynamic of relations between and among states. For just war thinkers, peace is not the absence of conflict, but the existence of a just order. Thus, the Middle East was not "at peace" before the onset of the Gulf War. It was caught in the grip of a violent order—Iraq under Saddam Hussein being one, perhaps the most egregious, case in point of a disordered state in the region—defined by injustices of the most grievous sort, as documented by such international human rights groups as Amnesty International and Middle East Watch. No state 'scapes whipping when measured up against strong standards of justice. But just war deplores creating false equivalencies: there is a big difference between being paid low wages for hard work; being denied the franchise; and being tortured or gassed because one's politics is "incorrect" or because one is a member of an ethnic minority which cannot defend itself against a dominant and violent majority.

The annexation of Kuwait by Iraq, the subsequent brutalization of Kuwaitis, and the gutting of their country were clear and blatant injustices, violations of basic principles of international order which encode respect for the autonomy of states. Allowing for the difficulties of getting accurate information from an occupied territory in time of war, evidence mounted rapidly of assassinations, torture, dispersal of populations, rape, sacking and pillaging—the whole panoply of the horrors of occupation by a hostile outside force.

What is remarkable about the subsequent response to Iraqi aggression is the way just war considerations framed so much of the debate. Here, the argument went, was a clear-cut case of unjust aggression: the paradigmatic instance of a *causus belli*. Responding to such aggression, in turn, fit the criterion of just cause. Sanctions were tried so that resort to war could be declared a last resort. Just war insists that war be declared by legitimate authority, and what could be more proper and more legitimate than a twenty-seven-nation coalition, acting under the imprimatur of the United Nations and in the name of collective security? Ticking off criteria for a *jus ad bellum* added up to a knockdown case for a defensive war to deny the fruits of

47

aggression to a dictator who tortured his own people and was certain to be even less cautious in his treatment of peoples of an occupied territory.

This, at least, is one plausible version of the story. But just war principles are ambiguous and complex. Evaluations have to be made at each step along the way. New facts may alter previous assessments. Greater and lesser evils must be taken into account. "The point about protecting a principle of order which honors sovereign boundaries is beyond dispute," according to Father Bryan Hehir, but this leaves us with "the crucial question" having to do "with proportionate means" ("Baghdad as Target: An Order to Be Refused," *Commonweal* [October 26, 1990], 603). What would be the cost of resisting *Iraqi aggression?* Would the postwar Gulf be a more, or less, unjust and disordered region? Might not the human and environmental damage, and the assaults to the spirit each and every war trails in its wake, blight *any* peace? The ends may be justified—restitutive response to aggression—but the means, the *jus in bello,* may be unjust or unjustifiable, even if pains are taken to avoid direct targeting of civilians.

Much of this complexity fell out of the argument in the weeks preceding the beginning of aerial bombardment and in the crucial early days of the war. Although the debate in the House of Representatives and the Senate was powerful and remarkable in many respects, the "just war discourse" that dominated the discussion was that of the President's. And the President was not in the least ambivalent. He declared the war just, as if this constituted both the beginning and the end of the matter. For President Bush, just war was a powerful instrument of legitimation for U.S. policy. But even if, as I have already suggested, a case for just cause could be made, it is troubling to see just war criteria brought forward and proffered as vindication for one side in so cavalier a manner: not so much wrapping oneself in the flag as in the moral mantle of purity. Just war warns against presumptions of moral triumphalism, beginning with St. Augustine's declaration that no earthly order is free from sin; hence, none dare equate itself with "the good" or "the just" unambiguously.

Crusaders of all stripes forget this lesson as they launch holy wars in which all right is on one side only. The Crusader promulgates a universe of Manichean absolutes: the Believer versus the Infidel. Forgetting that just war begins with a presumption against the use of force and then, with great reluctance, admits of possible exceptions to that rule, the crusader paints his opponent as the apotheosis of evil, the more readily to pave the way for an all-out effort to extirpate him, his ways, and all his works. Bush got some of the language and concerns of just war right and, his advisers insisted, he adhered to the doctrine that deadly force is always tragic even when it is necessary. But the tone and tenor of presidential rhetoric took off into the stratosphere of moralistic trumpeting of the sort just war cautions against. For example, the President spoke of "good versus evil, right versus wrong, human dignity and freedom versus tyranny and oppression." He equated our "just cause" with a "noble cause," a bit of crowing that more sober just war thinkers steadfastly avoided. The United States and its coalition were "on the side of God," he declared, although just war doctrine insists that God's ways are forever hidden to us in the temporal realm which is history and which all human beings inhabit.

To be sure, the President eschewed the most blatant excesses of crusading zeal in his care to distinguish the "brutal dictator, Saddam Hussein," nothing more nor less than a Hitler for our time, from the Iraqi people who were portrayed as his victims.[2] This distinction is vital and important

2. On Bush's just war doctrine, see Andrew Rosenthal, "Bush Vows to Tackle Middle East Issues," *The New York Times* (January 29, 1991), A13; Kenneth T.

within just war thinking, helping to forestall the vilification of entire nations and peoples. But given the intensity of the condemnation of Saddam, and the incessant upping of the rhetorical ante as a prelude to going to war and then as justification for having gone to war, much less attention got paid to such essential just war considerations as proportional response and the likely aftermath to a "victory" over Iraq for all the peoples of the region, including the citizens of Iraq.

Just war principles should never soothe; should always vex and trouble. But were we not soothed as we got reassured over and over again that civilian targets were not being hit? There is little doubt that the principle of discrimination was put into effect, with the assistance of laser technology, to achieve remarkably accurate targeting, against which the horror of the bombing of the shelter in Baghdad stands out in stark relief. If postwar estimates of noncombatant casualties of coalition bombing are at all accurate—five thousand to fifteen thousand civilians according to Greenpeace, a nonpartisan environmental group—that, surely, is something for which one can be grateful; if the bombing had been indiscriminate—as was the strategic terror bombing of civilian targets in World War II—civilian casualties would have been much higher. As Oliver O'Donovan put it, "Anyone may choose for himself whether he would prefer to have lived in Baghdad in January or in Hiroshima in August 1945 ("Were We Right to Fight?" *The Tablet* [June 15, 1991], 733). That the principle of discrimination, an aspect of classic just war teaching all but forgotten in this century's total wars, has been put back in place is all to the good if one holds that limiting the

Walsh, "Bush's 'Just War' Doctrine," *U.S. News and World Report* (February 4, 1991), 52–53; Kenneth L. Woodward, "Ancient Theory and Modern War," *Newsweek* (February 11, 1991), 47; Adam Nagourney, "Clerics Debate Whether War's 'Just,'" *USA Today* (January 29, 1991), 9A.

casualties and the lives lost is a priority of the most solemn sort.

But I worry that the *gravitas* that ought properly to attend any and all discussions of discrimination receded rather quickly, drowned out by crowing over "smart bombs" and overshadowed by repetitious instant replay of the bomb's-eye point of view as grainy black and white images imploded on our television screens. I don't doubt that the American people were smart enough to know they weren't watching a video game. But we were all rather stupefied by the insistence that "the experts," the techno-wizards and warriors, knew best all along: all that research and development had been worthwhile. Lives, and here American lives were, for the most part, the only explicit concern, were saved and our primacy as the world's greatest power reassured. Framed by celebrations of our know-how, the loss of life in the Baghdad bomb shelter became just a temporary blip on the screen. This tragedy *should* have been addressed by the President and our military spokesmen in language of deep regret and acknowledgment of responsibility—a responsibility ironically magnified precisely *because* our bombs were so "smart."

As well, because the media focused nearly all its concerns on whether or not noncombatants were the actual targets of coalition bombing strategy, the public's attention got deflected from the long-range effects of coalition bombing, including life-threatening assaults on the infrastructure of Iraqi society—energy and water supplies, communications, and other services. These are ambiguous matters within a just war framework. The hard-line realist can readily say, "Hit anything that makes them hurt and impairs their ability to make war." But the just war thinker must not move so hastily. He or she must sift out that which is vital to the opponent's war effort—including power and communications stations—and that which, while it may be drawn into support of military actions, is essential to sustain civilian life itself: here water and food supplies are foremost. Writes O'Donovan, "Water supplies are a paradigm for the most socially necessary of the infrastructure targets, which must be protected from attack if we are serious about making war on armies, not on populations" *(The Tablet,* 743). Everything that was hit could be said, in some sense, to be part and parcel of Iraq's long-range war-making capacity. But to say this, and nothing more, is to finesse rather than promote a wide-ranging debate on bombing strategy and how, save in the most vague sense, these targets were justified. An open just war debate requires explicit consideration of whether, for example, water reservoirs were directly targeted or not. But, postbellum, all is silent from those in power. A few mistakes are acknowledged, nothing more.

The First Geneva Protocol (1977) codifies just war thinking on civilian and nonmilitary targeting in language that directs our attention not just to the buildup to war, or the war itself, but to its long-term consequences. Those consequences now include malnutrition, even starvation, and epidemics linked directly to tainted and inadequate food and water supplies and medicines. A Harvard study estimates that some 170,000 children will die from delayed effects of the war. This figure is awfully high, but whatever the final toll, many thousands of children are certain to become casualties of war postbellum. Just war argument precludes a punitive peace. There is little justice, and much that smacks of punishment, in the suffering of the Iraqi people in the war's aftermath. If, as the President insisted, they are Saddam Hussein's victims, too, it is blatantly inconsistent with just war as politics to torment this people further in order to bring the dictator to heel. The war did not dislodge him. A just peace must not try to do so over the malnourished bodies of Iraqi children.

My point is that just war thinking must not be hauled out

on various rhetorical or ceremonial occasions and then shelved once the rhetorical or political moment has passed, or the case made. If just war is evoked, as the President and many of our opinion leaders evoked it, then they should stay within the framework they have endorsed. The health catastrophes faced by the Iraqi public; the desperate plight of the Kurds, made more desperate by continued economic sanctions and by our failure to intervene early and massively with humanitarian aid and protection from Saddam's forces; the released estimates showing that 100,000 Iraqi soldiers were killed and 300,000 wounded—all of this leaves one uneasy. And it should.

For another just war criterion, proportionality, suggests that the extraordinary lopsidedness of deaths and casualties tells us something: that excessive firepower may have been used, well past the point when the Iraqi army was in any position to resist. It tells us that the pounding of ill-armed, ill-clad, and ill-fed Iraqi soldiers was without mercy. It tells us that the carnage of the "Highway of Death," as desperate Iraqis were relentlessly bombed and strafed as they fled a country they had pillaged and attempted to destroy ecologically and economically as well as politically, was not a fight by *jus in bello* standards but a massacre, for those incinerated had no capacity to fight back. Just war teaching is lodged in a tradition which insists that justice must be tempered with mercy and that, in morally ambiguous situations, one should take a gamble on erring on the side of mercy.

No one can fight a war without getting blood on his hands. But, surely, more died and bled than need have. And where is just war talk from the President now? In justifying our policy of too little, too late toward the Kurds, the President seemed to forget just war considerations, repairing instead to the language of strategy, diplomacy, and pragmatic refusal to "intervene" in the internal affairs of another nation.

53

But since the President had a rather big hand in bringing about those internal affairs, surely this rhetoric falls short and falls flat. To move from a near crusade to a prudent realism creates an ethical schism of precisely the sort just war politics aims to heal or to bridge.

Just war offers no definitive answer to the question "But was it just?"—at least not as I understand its requirements. Just war thinkers will differ in their answer to that question. The important point for contemporary civic life is that just war imposes constraints where they might not otherwise exist; it generates a debate that might not otherwise occur; and it promotes ongoing skepticism and queasiness about the use and abuse of power without opting out of political reality altogether in favor of utopian fantasies and projections. It requires action and judgment in a world of limits, estrangements, and partial justice, and it fosters recognition of the provisionality of all political arrangements. It is at once respectful of distinctive and particular peoples and deeply internationalist. It recognizes self-defense against unjust aggression but refuses to legitimate imperialistic crusades and the building of empires in the name of peace when there is no peace.

There is more. I noted earlier that just war thinking is about far more than war. It includes a vision of "domestic" politics as well and of what the justice of a political order might be. Just war argument sustains a worldview that construes human beings as innately and exquisitely social. It follows that all ways of life are laced through with moral rules and restrictions that provide a web of social order. For St. Augustine, the entire sentient human race belonged within one category, the human, for God created us all: male and female, all races, all the wondrous diversity within the unity of creation. God's natural law was written in human hearts; thus, unsurprisingly, all ways of life incorporate basic grammars of injunctions and prohibitions which regulate important things—the taking of human life, sexual relations, the administration of justice. Rather than bifurcating human life into public and private realms, with rules of behavior appropriate to each, Augustine finds in the household the beginning of the city: What happens in families bears a reference to what sort of society one lives in overall; domestic peace and civic peace are related, are of a kind, rather than being entirely separable concerns. We can assess a people and a way of life by looking at what this people lifts up and loves; by what it shares in common, and by what it rejects or thrusts aside.

If, as I have claimed, just war incorporates a wider theory of a just politics and if, as I have argued, that politics rests on a recognition of our sociality and on the essential integrity of human relationships at the most fundamental levels of families, friendships, and communities, it follows that political actions and public policies can and must be assessed by looking at their impact upon families and communities, by examining what effect these policies have on our most vital and fragile human relationships. Just war as politics embraces a standpoint: the standpoint of the child and the child's needs and it requires that one evaluate periods of "peace" as well as times of "war" with reference to minimal requirements of both justice and mercy.

This brings me to the matter of "our men and women in the Gulf." During and after the war, we heard a lot about the "historic turnabout" on the issue of women in war and about the final defeat of various myths—that women are weaker, need protecting, are physically incapable of handling combat, and so on. According to proponents of women-in-combat and of waiving in future wars the combat exclusion rule, current laws and restrictions are about one thing only—denial of equal opportunity, preventing women from promotions and career progression. On one of the many radio interview programs I participated in during the

Gulf War, I suggested that perhaps we Americans should be thinking about what happens to the very young children, some of them infants of six weeks, whose mothers (sometimes a child's only parent) are deployed to a war zone: this is a matter of simple justice and humanity, I argued. I was told in no uncertain terms by the other participant on the program, an officer in a major national women's rights organization, that I was "reducing women to a uterus." That seems to be the level to which our political discourse in this matter has fallen.

If just war counts among its aims the enhancement of the quality of debate over such monumental questions as war and justice, it also can be drawn upon to challenge the narrow construals which dominate our domestic political discourse. Rights. Equality of Opportunity. Power. I am dubious that the reality of mothers separated from newborns and a burnishing of the glamour of military life, now as women's work, can or should be interpreted solely in the language of individualism and careerism. This is an impoverished ethical and political vocabulary. Just as realpolitik with its hard-edged notion of sovereignty and force impoverishes our understanding of the world of nations, so the language of rights as entitlements, if it is our exclusive language for "domestic politics," impairs our ability to think clearly about men, women, and children and the complexities of their lives. My reservations are not about female ability but about what gets glossed over, devalued, and diminished if our sole concern in the matter of women and war is with yet another incantation against the "glass ceiling" to women's advancement.

First, a brief reprise of the facts. Women were 6 percent of the overall force in Operation Desert Storm, some 32,350 of a total force of about 540,000. The staccato repetition of "our men and women in the Gulf" by the media tended to disguise the lopsidedness of the rotation in favor of men.

Depending upon how one counts war and war-related deaths, the number of female casualties was from 5 to 10 total—the "ultimate sacrifice," as we continue to refer to wartime loss. Women served as supply pilots, mechanics, police officers, ordnance workers (putting bomb payloads into planes); and the usual array of clerical, nursing, and support services. Women did not serve and, as of this writing, cannot serve in ground combat, on warships, or as pilots of attack planes. But every other "job description" is up for grabs.

The Gulf War not only put women in uniform closer to combat than ever before in our history; but it also marked a definitive signal that the United States is willing to put more women officially in war danger zones than is any other country. Israel, for example, often thought of as a country with "women soldiers," exempts all married women from the military and reserves, and women in the Israel Defense Forces have no combat duties on land or sea. Opposition in Israel to positioning women near the front lines is very strong. Contemporary American society is divided in this matter. Although 74 percent of women and 71 percent of men, according to an NBC/*Wall Street Journal* poll, favored sending women on combat missions, 64 percent of Americans overall rejected sending mothers of young children into the war zone. Military women, too, are divided. Those with career aspirations in the military are eager to waive any and all combat exclusion clauses. But other women, primarily noncareerists in the reserves, harbor doubts. In other words, those most in favor of women in combat are those most likely to benefit directly from earning their stripes in combat. Unsurprisingly, it was these women who were most often quoted and celebrated in war and postwar media hype.

Just war politics—being a theory of just politics grounded in our irreducible sociality—directs our attention away from glamorous images of women posed with M-16s to the image of desperate reservists separated from infants. Remember Specialist 4th Class Hollie Vance bidding her seven-week-old daughter good-bye? She said she had never anticipated combat, "let alone right after I had my first child. I've built an ice wall around my heart to try to cool the pain." The quality of mercy is strained, and broken, at such harsh severing of the fundamental human tie between a mother and an infant. The Gulf War left children from 17,500 families "without the custodial single parent who usually cares for them or without both parents, according to Defense Department figures," noted *The Washington Post* for February 15, 1991. Many mothers balked at going. One mother of a twenty-one-month-old child and a five-month-old nursing baby pled to be able to wean her baby, "but they said no . . . It's a nightmare" *(The New York Times* [January 31, 1991]). Another mother, Faith Stewart, got her orders and went into labor the next day. "It's outrageous to separate a mother and her new baby," she claimed.

There were, of course, the usual handwringing reports during the war of children's lives disrupted, of aggression, jitters, sleeplessness, kids blaming themselves for their parents' absence, kids traumatized by being uprooted from their neighborhoods and communities—but we seem to have grown insensitive to all that. There is so much pain in so many places and, besides, aren't we talking about a fundamental "right" when it comes to women fighting wars? Just war politics suggests that we back off rights absolutism, whether it comes burnished as feminism or not, and that we consider the sobering possibility that a society that puts the needs of its children dead last is a society "progressing" rapidly toward moral ruin.

For just war thinkers, peace is the fruit of justice. And justice is a vision of a balanced order, a world in which human dignity is the touchstone of public policy; a world in which the needs of the human being, at each stage of the life cycle, are recognized and respected; a world in which responsibility and rights go hand in hand. As we draw up the balance sheet in the matter of the Gulf War, whose effects will be felt for years to come, we must do so not only in mind of the strategic brilliance of the Desert Storm campaign, with its remarkable tote sheet "in our favor" on all counts, including combatant lives, but also in mind of malnourished Iraqi children; alongside breaking the war machine of an aggressive and despotic power, we must weigh the breaking of fundamental human relationships, some at their most fragile point, in the early weeks and months of lives as parents, especially mothers, and children were separated; in the same breath as we marvel over the peaceful taking and decent treatment of thousands of Iraqi prisoners of war, we must recount, with appropriate unease, the frenzied destruction of defenseless Iraqis on the "Highway of Death."

The celebrations are over. The bands have played. The soldiers have marched. The confetti has fallen, creating multicolored drifts on city streets. Now is the time to get sober and to remember what St. Augustine taught: war and strife, however just the cause, stir up temptations to ravish and to devour, often in order to ensure peace. Just war is and must remain a cautionary tale of internal and international order, a story of the requirements and purposeful uses of power and order, a lens through which to look at the heart of what constitutes peace. The earthly city is never free from the dangers of bloodshed, sedition, and war. A human being cannot even be certain of "his own conduct on the morrow," let alone specify and adjudicate that of others in ways he or she foreordains. In this world of discontinuities and profound yearnings, of sometimes terrible necessities, a human being can yet strive to maintain or to create an order that approximates justice, to prevent the worst from happening, and to resist the seductive lure of imperial grandiosity.

In his classic work, *Democracy in America,* Alexis de Tocqueville warned that military greatness was pleasing to the imagination of a democratic people. He feared the ephemeral but corrupting luster of such greatness. So does the just war thinker. He or she points us to other stories— stories of children at play without fear, of parents seeing their grandchildren born, of life's passages marked by kin and friends, in neighborhoods and towns and great cities. Sharing in such moments offers us what St. Augustine called "the delightfulness of peace," and it is that delight, by contrast to war's grandeur, that lies at the heart of just war thinking.

CAN WARS
BE JUST?

A Palestinian Viewpoint
of the Gulf War

SARI NUSSEIBEH

Was the Gulf War just? Can any wars be just? These questions about wars—as indeed about acts of force more generally—confront Palestinians not as academic questions but in their daily lives. On the one hand, we are faced by a military power which justifies its forceful occupation of our lands by an appeal to a religious argument: that God promised this land to Jews. On the other hand, we are ourselves motivated to resist this occupation partly by an appeal to a moral principle: that a people has a right to be free on its land.

Every time an act of violence occurs, whether it perpetuates the occupation or tries to put an end to it, someone can be found who will take the issue back to its moral or religious roots. The readiness with which such justifications occur tempts one to wonder if moral and religious principles have not been invented in the first place to justify the use of force in the pursuit of interests. True, moral arguments for

61

the use of force may not be persuasive, but perhaps their real function anyhow is less to persuade others of one's rights than to persuade them that the motivation for using force is the conviction that one is right. By thus elevating their motives, human aggressors may hope to distinguish themselves from other members of the bestial kingdom. Typically in such circumstances, in any case, it is not by the power of moral reasoning that such aggressors aim to achieve their objectives, but by the power of force. Moral and religious arguments are used to camouflage this evil beneath the veneer of pure intent.

Such cynicism about justifications of war and violence stems from being a witness to how much cruelty can be inflicted behind the masks of religion and morality. Under occupation, Palestinians watch how the religious imperative for settlement in God's land dispossesses people of their homes, of their lands and crops, of their freedoms, and sometimes even of their lives. In the course of twenty-five years of occupation, more than 60 percent of the land has been confiscated; thousands of homes have been demolished, thousands have been expelled from their homeland, thousands of crops and trees have been uprooted; long and total curfews have been imposed on villages, towns, and even whole areas; schools and universities have been shut down; a quarter of a million cases of arrest have been recorded, and thousands have been killed. It is a miracle in such circumstances not to be cynical. For the choice is between cynicism and pain—not only the physical pain that one suffers, but the intellectual pain of awareness. For some, perhaps what is most painful about being a Palestinian is the constant consciousness of injustice as a way of life. Yet it is such pain, rather than cynicism, that keeps hope aglow. For it is a constant reminder of being human in the face of an unscrupulous process of dehumanization.

CAN WARS BE JUST?

One day recently I watched as an Israeli soldier manhandled a Palestinian pedestrian in a street in the West Bank town of Ramallah. There was a disturbance somewhere in the town, and soldiers were running around the streets ordering shop owners to close down and go home. Loudspeakers were declaring the imposition of a curfew. In the midst of this tense atmosphere, two soldiers had pinpointed one pedestrian on whom they wished to demonstrate the absolute supremacy of the military. I watched from a window on the fourth floor, passively registering the events unfolding before my eyes. It was not a dramatic scene by any account. The soldiers did not fire at the Palestinian. They did not use the butts of their rifles. And eventually the Palestinian was let free. There was no need to record the event in the annals of the occupation's mistreatment of Palestinians. This was not newsworthy. In fact, the event was eerily commonplace. As one of the soldiers stood by, the other was shouting threateningly at the man, telling him that he should be off the streets. The Palestinian, powerless and conscious of his unfortunate role as the unwilling guinea pig on whom a lesson was to be demonstrated, was pleading the case that he had not yet had time to comply with the curfew order—it had in fact just been announced, and the streets were still fairly full, with people hurriedly finishing off their business before shutting up and going home. But the soldier was not prepared to listen to any argument or explanation. Whether consciously or unconsciously, he was at that moment intent on enacting a special assignment, namely, the demonstration that Palestinian reasoning, whatever heights it may reach, does not rise to the level of Israeli force. Every time the Palestinian opened his mouth to say something, the soldier, who had him gripped with one arm, slapped him fully in the face with his other hand. This was a history lesson, a lesson in intimidation, a lesson in how to demean human

63

dignity and pride, a lesson in the worthlessness of being a Palestinian. The Palestinian seemed to me to be pitiably cowering, while the soldier stood menacingly tall. I had seen such lessons being taught under occupation in more than one form, in more than one place, on more than one occasion. But I could not overcome my feeling of pain. I was fully conscious of beholding reality at its ugliest.

Human psychology has built-in self-defense mechanisms. When the consciousness of injustice is so commonplace, pain is often turned inward, subterfuged by a sense of cynicism. One programs one's expectations to suit the situation, and is therefore always ready and waiting for the next event.

It was 11:30 P.M. when soldiers, having surrounded the house, knocked on my door. It was January 29, thirteen days since the aerial bombardment in the Gulf War had started. For fully two weeks we had been placed under a total twenty-four-hour curfew, interspersed only by three two-hour intervals in which we were allowed to do our shopping. All of us—my wife, my three children, and myself—had taken to sleeping together on the floor of the sitting-dining area of our apartment. This way we kept each other company through the Scud scares (yes, even we Palestinians felt tense whenever the sirens blew, as we wondered each time where the rockets would fall, and what deadly poison they might be carrying). During that period a kind of primeval debate about the good and evil forces of history had become common, inspired in part by the moralizing speeches of some of the world leaders engaged in this war. Ordinary people also seemed to have an urgent need to moralize their emotions and attitudes. I was inundated with telephone calls, some of them from Israeli or Western journalists demanding that I condemn the missile attacks on Israel. It felt like a morality test—as if I was being subjected to some kind of moral blackmail. There were good forces and evil forces. The good forces fired good missiles that had to be condoned. The evil forces fired evil missiles that had to be condemned. On which side was I? I refused to make the distinction. It seemed to me that there was something absurd about it, even grotesque. I felt infuriated by the questions. The entire war was condemnable, it seemed to me, and within that context also the entirety of the missiles, regardless of color or origin.

For almost two weeks we lived in a state of suspension between TV scenes of missiles hitting Iraqi targets and footage of missiles flying over our heads. We were but one family in a population of 1.5 million Palestinians who had been confined to their homes. But Palestinian sufferings and fears were not aired on TV screens during that period—only the children giving vent to their primitive instincts of joy as missiles of destruction missed them and flew toward the enemy.

At 11:30 P.M. all of us were still awake. We often stayed up till the early hours of the morning, sometimes taking turns at being awake, glued to our television set, watching for news or trying to kill the hours of the night. The children quickly and matter-of-factly informed me of the identity of the visitors. None of us were surprised. We all knew that the time had come, and that it was now my turn. Ever since the intifada started, we had expected to hear such a knock. There had been tens of thousands of cases of arrest over the previous three and a half years. Two of the soldiers—rather politely and unenthusiastically, it seemed to me—handed me a detention order signed by the Minister of Defense. For state security reasons I had to be placed under administrative detention for six months at Ramleh (Nissan) jail. As the soldiers calmly waited, my wife and children quickly and efficiently packed a small suitcase for me. Jamal, my eldest son, took care to include *The Hitchhiker's Guide to the Galaxy*, Volume 1—a science fiction novel which proved to be excellent reading during the first hours of isolation inside a prison cell. The children came down to see me off as I was led into the back of one of the five Jeeps waiting around the house. Lassie, a handsome, black, part–German shepherd, barked ferociously at all the excitement. This was the only hint of commotion. Otherwise it was dead silent. Even the soft drizzle that had begun to fall did not make a sound. The eerie silence gave the operation a dreamlike quality, compounding my sense of apprehension as I crossed the threshold away from the only reality I knew. Later that night, sitting alone in the dimly lit holding cell of the Russian Compound jail in Jerusalem (where I was to await my transportation to Ramleh) and trying to take in my new situation, I heard the Hebrew news from a radio next door. The media campaign against me had started: I was an Iraqi spy, a Scud specialist, some kind of human rocket-guiding system. The detention order signed by the Minister had been general and noncommittal. The statements now made by various officials on the radio were specific and truly terrifying. I could see my public image totally crumble before Israeli eyes. Years of dialogue with Israelis, of confidence building, of trying to create understanding were now systematically demolished by the radio broadcasts. I felt totally helpless and stuck, unable to respond to the media charges. (These charges would grow in the following days into accusations by one of Israel's top-ranking spokesmen that I was in charge of an entire spy ring which had been rounded up and was under interrogation.)

It was not until 4 P.M. on the following afternoon that a lawyer was allowed to see me. With sirens blowing and Scuds falling, with front-page news carrying the incredible fabrications and charges, I felt totally helpless. The lawyer informed me that the prosecution had to bring me before the court within the next twenty-four hours in order to confirm the detention order. But he also informed me that lawyers are not able in such cases to see, let alone to study, the evidence being brought against their clients. Just as state security reasons are cited for the detention order itself, state security reasons are also cited for keeping the alleged evidence a state secret.

I told my lawyer not to be intimidated by the prosecution's citing of "secret evidence"—I assured him there was none. None of the media charges against me were true, I told him. My only mistake had been to provide an excuse for the authorities by answering a telephone call from someone who said that he was the Iraqi Ambassador to Tunis. I spoke to the caller in the polite manner that I would use with any journalist or caller—even Israeli—who is interested in hearing my views. Whatever facts I used for my individual assessment and opinions concerning the overall situation were in any case public knowledge acquired from the media. I had said nothing to the man that I did not say, or could not have said, to absolutely anyone who called me during that period to inquire about our condition and my views. But I had given the authorities the chance they had been waiting for.

In the days that followed, a deal was struck between the lawyers and the prosecution. On my part, I would refrain from taking the matter up in the High Court. On theirs, they would reduce the detention by three months. I accepted because, given the atmosphere of the time, I calculated that I would not get a sympathetic hearing, no matter how fabricated the charges were. The damage to my image was already done. I was bowing to what I knew was an injustice.

During the following three months, sharing a tiny two-by-three-meter self-sufficient cell with one other Palestinian detainee, being confined inside it for twenty-three hours a day (for one hour we were allowed to go out to exercise in a yard), I was surprised to discover how free I had become. Deprived of all external commitments, responsibilities, or pursuits, I became free to reenter an intellectual universe I had almost forgotten existed, to rethink subjects which the mundane but overwhelming and oppressive routine of daily life had totally submerged. This spiritual freedom enabled me to be pure and genuine in the formation of my thoughts and attitudes, and I felt, paradoxically in that condition, that I possessed far more strength than my jailors—not the prison guards, but their masters who plotted my confinement.

Externally, this new sense of purity reflected itself in the ability to take full cognizance of my cellmate—a journalist who was undergoing his third spell of administrative detentions since the intifada began three and a half years earlier. Not since my youth have I been able to look into and appreciate another human being, to be amazed by his inner riches, to feel the true closeness of friendship. In the adjoining cell a Palestinian psychologist—a graduate of a school in the Soviet Union—was awaiting trial on charges of belonging to one of the PLO factions (it was amusing to hear him converse on occasion with one of the prison guards, a Russian immigrant, in Russian).

Also, being free to look into myself, I felt curiously closer to God. I read my scripture (the Qur'an) with a deeply strengthened moral and intellectual sense. The scriptural message was never as transparent to me as it was then. More than at any other time, I felt the unity of the Abrahamic message of Judaism, Christianity, and Islam. I reflected on how ironic it was that this message of God had been scattered and squandered by the bigotry of His religion's zealot practitioners.

I also had ample time in jail to reflect on the Palestinian predicament and on good and evil missiles. By a strange coincidence, one of the books my wife had packed for me was Tolstoy's *War and Peace.* I therefore also had time to reflect on the nature of wars: how they are willed and pursued. I was grateful when, on coming out of jail, I was given the opportunity in this volume to contribute some preliminary thoughts on the subject.

I must confess that I had not thought through the issue of the justness of force until this opportunity came. Being naturally inclined against the use of force, I had simply assumed myself to be a pacifist. However, on considering the matter, I discovered that I am not a pure pacifist. Let me introduce my thoughts on the subject by beginning with some of my conclusions. It seems to me that if there are just wars, then they exist mostly in theory and rarely if ever in the real world. Moreover, while many just war theorists are undoubtedly genuine, more often than not such theories are exploited by ruthless men who knowingly prosecute wars in the pursuit of their interests. Thus one finds very often that moral arguments for the justification of the use of collective violence are cosmetic constructs used either to drum up support for, or to silence (potential or actual) opposition to, an action whose real motivation is the fulfillment of a perceived interest. Sometimes—perhaps the Gulf War is an example—the prosecutors of war fall victim to the delusion that the war they wish to prosecute is indeed a paradigm of the just war theory. This is a real tragedy: Given that moral systems and religious perspectives often vary, we find that history is replete with examples of wars in which the antagonists feel equally self-righteous. As I shall try to show, the antagonists in the recent Gulf War at least tried to exhibit outwardly the signs of being self-righteous about their actions.

I tried hard to discover what my own attitude is toward war and violence. In doing so, I had to inquire a little further than some of the criteria normally used to define when a war can be just (availability of options, proportionality, level of civilian casualties, the probability of success, the speed with which success could be achieved, and the like). It seemed to me that a large number of these criteria were in any case *secondary* in the following sense: that one has to determine, first, whether any action of collective violence is morally acceptable, and second, whether this specific action of collective violence is morally motivated. The assumption here is that if it can be established at all that such acts are morally acceptable, then they must be morally motivated. This is like saying that a moral act must fulfill subjective as well as objective conditions. If what I called "secondary" criteria are objective or relate to objective conditions, the "moral motivation" of an act describes a subjective state and is to my mind a necessary condition for an act's moral acceptability. Turning specifically to wars, and assuming them generally to be cases where force is used by formal political entities (and thus excluding for the moment such categories as national liberation wars or civil wars, where the polities in question may not be "formal"—for example, where they may not be recognized members of the United Nations), I asked myself the basic question of whether such force can be justified. To help myself answer this question, I tried to determine whether I would find the use of force on the smaller scale of individuals justifiable. My assumption here—misleading, as it turned out—was that if force can be justified against individuals, it can also be justified against formal political entities. Once I formulated the question in this manner, it seemed that I could easily imagine situations where I would feel the use of force or coercion justifiable. The obvious examples were cases when force is used in self-defense in life-threatening situations, or where criminals are punished by law through coercion of some kind, or even where, in extreme cases, corrective coercion is used in the upbringing of children (or the training of animals).

So I had to confront the conclusion that I was not the pure pacifist I might have imagined myself as being. I thought that I could more aptly describe myself as a relative pacifist (or someone who thinks that, while as a standard rule force ought not be used, there are nevertheless cases where extenuating circumstances might legitimize its use). I admit to having worried at that instant about calling the use of force in such cases "just." But then, reminding myself that a court of justice, in redressing certain wrongs, enacts coercive punishment whose very essence is justice, I concluded that I cannot escape the fact that the use of force or coercion can indeed sometimes be described as just.

In other words, in trying to answer the basic question "Is the use of force ever justified?" I found myself saying yes, with qualifications. From here, and as a self-confessed nonpacifist, I had to turn to other important questions, namely, how to determine who has the right to enact coercive action and under what conditions such action can be described as just.

It is at this point that one runs the risk of using misleading assumptions: I had started out by wishing to determine whether the use of collective violence is justifiable at all, and I imagined that I could answer this question by determining more specifically my attitude toward the use of force against individuals. Now that I had determined for myself that the use of force against individuals is justifiable under certain conditions, I thought I could easily and by analogy see how on the level of formal political entities the use of force can be justified—the example of Hitler seemed perfect in the context. Indeed, many of us tend instinctively to say that if force is justifiable at all, then surely it is a simple matter to see how it can be justified when used in wars. More specifically, one tends to say that if coercive action can be justified in the context of, say, democratic societies for the protection of the rights of their individual members, then surely an analogous argument can be made for the use of such action

71

in the international context for the protection of the rights of sovereign countries. However, such assumptions and analogies, while seeming innocuous, turn out in fact to be fallacious, and the Hitler example proves to be the exception rather than the rule.

Simply put, the problem with the reasoning I had employed is that the world is not a democratic society, neither in terms of the identity of its formal members nor in terms of the international relations which hold between them. Democratic societies consist of individuals who are bound together through their consent and will, and who have established through this joint will, among other things, a juridical system which has as its aim the enforcement of the law in that society, thus ensuring the rights and safety of its individual members. However, the analogy between individuals in such a society and formal political entities like the member states of the United Nations breaks down as soon as it is scrutinized. The first and fundamental asymmetry consists in the fact that, unlike ordinary individuals, each of whom is a natural entity, formal political entities are historical constructs whose identity and territory have been established through some measure of force. Thus, while individuals are identifiable as distinct entities by right of birth, formal political entities are identifiable units not by virtue of birth but due to a complicated interplay of the forces of history—an interplay in which justice rarely takes part.

This distinction between individual and formal political entity reflects itself today in the fact that not all existent formal political entities are indeed internally unified or sufficiently cohesive (as witness the cases of Yugoslavia and the Soviet Union). Furthermore, the difference between individuals and the contrived composition of most formal political entities is also reflected in the converse fact that not all aspiring national groups are enabled in the world of today to become formal political entities, but are in fact kept stateless by power and force (as witness the cases of the Palestinians and the Kurds). Thus it is not by virtue of birth or free will that a national group becomes a formal political entity, or fails to become so, but most often by power and force.

Furthermore, one finds that the borders of some formal political entities have been delineated by foreign powers in the course of establishing postbellum spheres of influence (as the Austrian or Iraqi-Kuwaiti borders); while other formal political entities (for example, Israel) have so far refrained from formally delineating their borders in expectation of some advantageous bargaining positions which reflect the balance of power and the results of war. To observe all these facts is not even to make a statement yet about whether national groups have analogous rights as individuals to be "formal political entities": It is simply to draw attention to the vast distinction between individuals and formal political entities, and to the mistake therefore of assuming that what is morally acceptable for the former must automatically be acceptable for the latter. In this kind of situation it becomes obvious that the legitimacy of the existence of sovereign countries who are member states of the United Nations is more a reflection of balances of power than of natural rights. It is hardly surprising in this kind of context, therefore, to find that the relations between states which are formalized in the political aggregate called "the United Nations" are totally unlike those existing among individuals in a democratic society, because these international relations are entirely rooted in force and in the possession of power. Thus, the enfranchisement of national groups is only endowed to a few rather than to all; and once the huff and puff of the leaders of the small member states dies down, there can only be one Caesar. Thus we also find that the United Nations General Assembly is powerless constitutionally before the main ruling club, namely the Security Council, while we find the latter a mere instrument of the world's military powers—lately, of *the* superpower, the United States.

The real problem therefore lies in the nature of world relations, where not all are equal before the law, and where, instead of power being the instrument of law, it is the law which is the instrument of power. It is this anomaly that makes truly moral wars a rarity, and that reveals the United Nations–sponsored Gulf War as a war conceived and orchestrated by only one country, the United States, which was enabled to perform this deed not because it stood for what is right but because it was the superpower. Indeed, the distinctions on the one hand between natural individuals and formal political entities, and on the other between the parliamentary system that binds individuals together in a democratic society and an international system of relations which reflects the balances of power between states, make it extremely difficult if not often farcical to speak about justifiable coercive action by states in fulfillment of United Nations resolutions. The difficulty was obvious in the recent war when the United States stopped short of helping the Kurds achieve independence in Iraq. For where is the justice in the refusal of the United States, because of a professed concern for the territorial integrity of Iraq, to help the Kurds achieve their independence, when the obvious criterion for this policy is that Iraq is a formal political entity while the Kurds, through forces of history, have not achieved this status? The whole matter becomes farcical when one considers that, while the issue of Kurdish independence was at least broached in relation to Iraq, it was never even mentioned in relation to the U.S. ally Turkey (where the majority of the Kurds live and the bulk of Kurdistan lies). Obviously, what guided the U.S. actions was not a true system of justice but an international realpolitik which makes a sham of such actions.

In an ideal world, where all (and only) naturally deserving and desiring national groups are recognized formal members of a world political body, where mutual recognition is reached by a system of consent, where each formal political entity is equal before a single unifying law whose purpose is to protect the rights of all, where member states have thus consented to transferring their right to self-protection to the body politic as a whole—where, in a word, a democratic society among nations truly exists—it is possible then to determine with clarity and precision when an injustice has been committed and when an act of war is therefore justifiable. In an imperfect world, on the other hand, one has to take care lest morality is invoked, not as the primary motivation for an action, but as an afterthought, even perhaps as a psychological weapon to reinforce the destructive capabilities of a country's military arsenal as it decides to engage in a war in pursuit of its interests.

This does not mean that, in the absence of a perfect international order, wars can never be justified. That would be far too idealistic a position to take. However, a Platonic perspective helps to keep one's judgments on real-world wars under control. Surely infringements on the rights of individuals, national groups, and states are rampant in the world. One cannot wait for a perfect world order before one acts to redress a particular injustice. There must be intervention. However, for such intervention to be just, and before even the objective criteria for determining its justness are brought to bear, it must be established that the intervention was morally motivated—that is, that its aim was the upholding of natural rights and moral principles. These are not inscrutable, and paradoxically many of them are contained in the United Nations charters. "International legitimacy" cannot be a substitute for these when it is simply a code word for the restoration of an unjust state of affairs whose primary function is to serve the interests of the intervening party. For in the Gulf situation, Iraq's occupation of Kuwait was but one injustice among many. Further political injustices abound within the two countries, as within other countries in the region—whether having to do with systems of government, or treatment of minorities, or distribution of wealth, or issues of human rights, or even issues of borders.

Speaking generally, the moral credibility of an intervention can only be established if there is at least a demonstrated resolve to address the underlying causes of injustice, regardless of the effects this may have on the interests of the intervening party. Moreover, the moral credibility of the intervening party also has to be established. This is not a necessary condition for a moral intervention, but it is an important consideration given the nature of behavioral patterns. The moral credibility of the intervening party can be established by determining, among other things, its consistency in dealing with cases of injustice. The requirement here is not necessarily that the intervenor deal with all cases of injustice before it can be justified in dealing with one such case; rather, it is that the country apply the same standards when and if it engages in dealing with more than a single case. The employment of double standards in this context immediately raises serious doubts about the moral credibility of the actor. Moral credibility (of the action as well as of the actor) can only be determined through practice. It is not impossible to determine whether the action of any party is motivated by a moral principle. Moral behavior is not inscrutable. It is as simple to see through the actions of governments as it is to see through the actions of individuals.

I would submit that in their respective actions (the occupation of Kuwait and its liberation), both Iraq and the

United States fail the moral credibility test in both of its aspects.

Two common themes pervade Iraq's occupation of Kuwait and the U.S. liberation of it: the application of force in the pursuit of self-interest, and the resort to an internal code of political and moral values as a justification for this.

Iraq's occupation of Kuwait was dictated by what was perceived as the need to fulfill certain financial and security requirements that did not seem forthcoming except through the use of force. The justification code used was complex, including the historical claim that the Iraq-Kuwait border was itself the result of a transaction dictated by force, the demographic claim that the Arab peoples are a single body disaggregated against their will, and the political claim that the occupation was a necessary prelude to the restoration of Palestinian rights.

The U.S. liberation of Kuwait was also dictated by what was perceived as the need to fulfill certain economic and security requirements that did not seem attainable except through the use of force: Iraq's military as well as geographic growth could only be regarded as causing a threat to the economic and security stability of the Gulf oil region, and, therefore, to the Western world. Once again, a complex moral camouflage was used to justify the force that was used to put an end to this threat. This camouflage included the claim that Iraq's occupation of Kuwait constituted "naked aggression" and infringed upon the very foundations of international legitimacy, the claim that the Iraqi regime is dictatorial—even reminiscent of Hitler's Nazi regime—and the claim that Kuwaiti women and children were being ravished by Iraqi troops.

While the moral and political claims of both parties were probably well founded, it is highly questionable whether it was the substance of these claims which constituted the motivation for the countries' respective actions. In the case of Iraq, a modus vivendi had evolved, even within the context of the Arab League, over the issue of there being a border with Kuwait, notwithstanding disagreements over its exact location. As for Arab unity or Palestinian rights, the Iraqi claims might have seemed more credible had there been signs of a more rigorous pursuit of such noble aims in advance of the Gulf crisis and Iraq's growing debts. In short, the "camouflage" nature of Iraq's moral and political justification of the occupation is obvious to the objective observer —although it was to some extent successful in the context of the Arab world.

Not so obvious, perhaps, was the analogous "camouflage" nature of the U.S.-led allies' moves. However, the irony of some of those claims was stunning, as when President Bush, holding hands (metaphorically) with Assad of Syria, enumerated the horrors and human rights violations being perpetrated by the enemy dictator Saddam. This hypocrisy was not missed in the Arab world. Other claims seemed equally hypocritical, as evidenced by such numerous blatant facts throughout the world as Israel's continuing occupation of territories recognized by the United Nations to belong to sovereign countries (Lebanon and Syria—both "formal political entities"), or the forced crushing of the uprising of the Baltic peoples even as the Gulf crisis was at its zenith, or the continued plight of women and children in countless places throughout the world, not least in the occupied Palestinian territories. Turning from questions about moral intent to objective criteria, the enormous human cost of civilian casualties still being paid by Iraqi women and children (with estimated expected number of deaths reaching 100,000) as a result of the continued embargo against Iraq is yet another mockery of the U.S. moral claims, and clearly violates the just war dictum against civilian casualties. Actually, one cannot at this stage even determine what the overall human cost of the war is going to be, especially to civilians who have had no part of it. How does one quantify the suffering of the hundreds of thousands of Palestinians, Kurds, Shiites, and Asians who were uprooted and compelled to migrate to different locations as a result of the war?

Finally, regarding the claim that through this war we have entered a new era of international legitimacy and an activation of the United Nations body in the settlement of world conflicts: This claim was thrown out the window as soon as the war ended and it became clear that, in addressing another world conflict in the same region, namely, the Israeli-Palestinian conflict, the United Nations body was no longer necessary but could be assigned a secondary role. Clearly, and despite the camouflage, the Security Council did not act as an independent body during the crisis; instead, it was turned into a pitiable and pliant factory for manufacturing resolutions that were dictated by the United States and that reflected U.S. policy and interests. Otherwise, how does one account for a dominant role for the United Nations in one instance but a totally subservient role in the next? Many of these observations (as well as others, like the U.S. opposition to a Security Council resolution that would have brought a United Nations–sponsored investigative commission to the Palestinian territories following a massacre in May 1990 when an Israeli shot seven Palestinian laborers on the street and nine more were killed in angry confrontations with soldiers during the rest of the day) detract from the moral credibility of the United States as an intervening party, as they mostly seem to indicate the use of double standards.

Furthermore, in acting to restore so-called "law and order," the United States had in fact mustered its military strength to restore what is essentially an unjust state of affairs. This state of affairs involves wide-ranging issues such as Iraqi claims on Kuwait (whether concerning debts, oil fields, or access to the Gulf), the Arab world's rights in the wealth of the Gulf region's oil, problems of human rights (whether in Iraq, Syria, or countries of the Gulf region), or problems of national minorities in the immediate vicinity. If the condition of moral credibility of a military intervention were to be upheld and satisfied, then the United States would have addressed those issues head-on; it would indeed have made its intervention contingent on some form of commitment by its Arab allies to redressing these injustices. It is precisely because the war failed to address those issues, and succeeded only in dealing with Iraq's occupation of Kuwait, that people now question the moral validity of the intervention. Because, while it is quite clear how the war resulted in benefits to the West and to the United States, it is not at all clear what benefits have accrued to the peoples of the region—except, of course, to members of the ruling dynasty of the Kuwaiti sheikhdom.

In short, the war was simply a display of force in the pursuit of an interest. The lesson learned by the average observer from the entire crisis (first the occupation and later the liberation) is as ugly as it is real: that what matters in the final analysis in such conflicts of interest is not which side is right and which side is wrong, but which world monster has longer and sharper teeth. If anything, the war was not a vindication of moral principles but a vindication of force. This may be a fact of history, but the United States—like the soldier in Ramallah—very dramatically demonstrated again this lesson to the world.

Perhaps not so oddly given their political history, Palestinians viewed the entire affair not from the perspective of hard-bitten interests but from that of moral and abstract political arguments. And given the nature of world politics, this was a sure recipe for another failure. Thus, rather than apply a calculus of interests in order to determine their positions (for example, to calculate whether it was for or against their interests to antagonize their main financial benefactor, namely, Saudi Arabia, or to alienate themselves from potential political supporters, namely, the Western countries), Palestinians formulated a position that was bound to please no one. They chose indiscriminately from the moral arguments used by Iraq and the allies: The occupation of Kuwait was wrong, they claimed, but so was the restoration of its undemocratic government. The use of force to erase unnatural borders separating different parts of the same Arab body was wrong, they claimed, but even more wrong was the forceful intervention of a non-Arab body to undo that erasure. Finally, even if Iraq was not genuine in its purpose to attack Israel, and even if it was deceitfully exploiting the Palestinian issue by trying to stir up Arab passions to break up the Arab coalition against it, nevertheless Iraqi Scud attacks against Israel were a sign of Arab military awakening and capability and a reminder of the ongoing issue of lost Palestinian rights.

A Palestinian position based on a pure cost-benefit calculus would have seen a symbolic PLO contingent fighting on the side of the allies. The PLO would have ensured a "respectable" place for itself in the emerging so-called "new world order." The approximately half million Palestinians living and working in the Gulf region would have been ensured stability and security (which are existential matters for a people living in exile without a homeland). The Palestinians under occupation would have continued receiving desperately needed funds from the Gulf countries (these, together with the income generated from trade with those countries, account for a full one third of the gross national income of the Palestinians in the Occupied Territories). And the PLO would have ensured continued financial support, especially from Saudi Arabia. The Palestinian failure to use this cost-benefit analysis is perhaps all the more striking since the PLO had no illusions about the outcome of the war. Arafat's efforts to the last minute were aimed at extricating Saddam from the confrontation, and the PLO relentlessly encouraged him to accept the last-minute efforts of France and of the Secretary-General of the United Nations to avert the war.

Yet, when things finally came to a head, Palestinians typically failed to determine their final course of action on the basis of their interests (had they been calculating and cynical, they could have justified doing so by a resort to the well-provided moral camouflage of the West). Instead, they formulated their positions in political abstraction and absolutist moral terms (as has been characteristic of them since the Balfour Declaration). The "moral" of this, to use a bitter term, is that the Palestinians have failed to evolve as an adept player in the international game of states. Obviously, to be an adept player like the United States is to know how to cloak purely interest-seeking actions in moral rhetoric and self-justification in such a way as to come out dominant in the end. And the secret of this success is not to take these justifications to heart. Once moral justifications and absolutist political standards are taken to heart, and are given priority over cold interests for guiding action, then the result in international politics is failure. This is perhaps the dilemma of Palestinian politics, and why the Palestinians have not succeeded yet in becoming one of the "respectable" formal political entities. For in the power-based world of these entities, morality is mostly a myth, and self-righteousness is mostly a cover for self-interest.

WHOSE
JUST WAR?
WHICH PEACE?

STANLEY HAUERWAS

The story is told of the "old boy" in Mississippi who was called to the ministry when he was out plowing with his mule. He interpreted a skywriter's "GP" as "Go Preach" rather than "Grand Prize Beer." Using his barn, he began to preach to whoever would come—black or white. Seeing nothing in the Gospels that required the separation of the races, he did not let threats from the Klan change his practice. As a result he was severely beaten. A friend who went to comfort him reported that he was undeterred by the beating since, as he said, "You know, there is a lot more to this race thing than just race."

In like manner there is a lot more to this "war thing" than just "just war." Indeed there is much more to the question of the moral evaluation of war than the question of whether a war conforms to just war criteria. Just as Christians think racism has to do with sin and repentance, so should we think of war. As will be clear from what follows, I certainly do not

83

mean to disparage all attempts to discipline and evaluate war on just war grounds. But rather I shall try to show how such attempts concerning the Gulf War have failed to acknowledge "the more."

"The more" to which I want to direct attention are the assumptions which have dictated, mistakenly in my view, what has become widely regarded as the relevant questions for assessing the morality of the Gulf War. Put differently, it makes all the difference who is asking questions about the "justice" of the war and for what reasons. When questions of who and why are ignored, the history that has shaped just war reflection as well as the conflicting histories of the Gulf War are assumed irrelevant.

Since I will argue that the "who" is all important, I must make clear who I am, or at least who I think I should be, and for whom I write. I am a Christian pacifist. From my perspective, that is an unhappy description since I believe the narrative into which Christians are inscribed means we cannot be anything other than nonviolent. In other words, Christians do not become Christians and then decide to be nonviolent. Rather, nonviolence is simply one of the essential practices that is intrinsic to the story of being a Christian. To "be Christian" is to be incorporated into a community constituted by the stories of God; as a consequence, this incorporation necessarily puts one in tension with the world that does not share those stories.

I write hoping to convince the many Christians who supported the Gulf War that such support was a mistake on Christian grounds. The so-called "just war theory," rather than helping Christians discern where their loyalties should be, in fact made it more difficult for Christians to distinguish their story from the story of the United States of America. As a result, appeals to the "just war theory" led to an uncritical legitimation of the Gulf War by most Christians in America. This should not be surprising since most Christians in America continue to imagine that this is a "Christian nation."

It may be suspected that as a pacifist I am trying to defeat the "just war theory" in principle by calling attention to its perversion in this instance. That is certainly not my intention. I do think the locution "just war theory" is misleading, since it not only presumes the theory has always had a coherence that it has in fact lacked, but more importantly it presumes that as a "theory" it can be used by anyone anywhere. Nonetheless, the question of whether a coherent and viable theory of just war can be defended on Christian grounds is separable from the question of whether the Gulf War conformed to just war criteria.

Yet I hope to show that these questions are in fact not so neatly separable if the just war theory is to avoid being used in an ideological fashion—that is, as a cover story that hides from us the reality of what was done in the Gulf War. And it is my contention that such a cover story is invoked whenever appeals to "just war theory" are used to create an illusory moral objectivity, as they have been in justifying the Gulf War.

For example, in one essay after another we have been reminded of the standard just war consensus: a just war is one declared by legitimate authority, whose cause is just, and whose ultimate goal is peace; furthermore, the war must be fought with the right intentions, with a probability for success, with means commensurate to its end, and with a clear respect for noncombatant immunity. Questions about the justice of the Gulf War seem to be a matter of whether "the facts" fit these criteria. It is assumed by those who defend the war on just war grounds and those who oppose the war on the same grounds that they are in fact standing on the same ground. The just war theory has become a given that can be generated and applied by anyone anywhere from any point of view.

But it is just this presumption that is the problem. The assumption that just war theory provides criteria of assessment that are straightforward, self-explanatory, and not requiring interpretation is, from a Christian perspective, a sinful illusion. It is the kind of illusion one has come to expect of those in modern societies who hide from themselves the violent nature of those societies by justifying them in "in principle" universalistic terms. Ironically, in such a context, it is left to the Christian pacifist to challenge such universalistic illusions by reminding those who would use the abstractions of just war theory that the wars of liberal societies, simply put, involve the use of violence for state interest. Such an illusion is sinful exactly because it hides from Christians our complicity in patterns of domination and violence.

That is why the title of this essay is a play on the title of Alasdair MacIntyre's book *Whose Justice? Which Rationality?* (Notre Dame: University of Notre Dame Press, 1988). MacIntyre's argument that, contrary to liberal pretentions of universality, all theories of justice and rationality are tradition-dependent is equally a challenge to the use of "just war theory" to justify the Gulf War. It has been the hallmark of ethical theory since the Enlightenment to ground morality in rationality qua rationality; in other words, morality only has meaning when considered as a schema of laws or principles that are supposedly self-evident to any reasonable person (thus the frequent invocation of the phrase "in principle"). But such accounts of morality, by their own admission, can only give extremely "thin" material content to their standards of right and wrong; they can proclaim that certain kinds of behavior are wrong "in principle." But when forced to consider added factors of a person's history, the circumstances of a situation, and the role of the community in an individual's life, these material conditions of morality are set aside in favor of simply asserting what "in principle" must be true anytime and anyplace. This loss of material content is a small price to pay for this assumed universality. The issue, then, for such systems of ethics becomes how such universally derived principles are to be applied in concrete cases.

Such theories of morality are attempting to free moral convictions from their history and, in particular, from their Jewish and Christian roots. From this perspective, for a principle to be moral it must be capable of being held and applied by anyone, whether they be Christian, Muslim, or American. It should not be surprising, therefore, that just war criteria were used to justify the Gulf War as if it made no difference who was using them and for what ends. It is my contention that when the just war theory is so used it cannot avoid ideological distortion.

The nature of such distortion is exemplified by what happens when I acknowledge that I write as a Christian pacifist in opposition to those who assume a just war stance. It is assumed that I am in a disadvantaged position because "pacifism," particularly a pacifism such as mine that is based on Christian beliefs, lacks "universal" or public standing because so few are thought to adhere to it and because of the religious commitment required. Thus even if I take up an analysis of the Gulf War, it is presumed that my arguments can only be persuasive to those in a community that worships God in the name of the Father, Son, and Holy Spirit.

It is certainly not my intention to deny that I write to, as well as from, a particular audience called Christian. Indeed my primary concern in this essay is to help Christians see how unfaithful we have been through our willingness to underwrite the ends of that entity called the United States of America. That I write with such purpose, however, does not mean that my argument is "limited" in ways that the argument of those who appeal to just war theory is not. Indeed it is my hope that non-Christians might be interested in the analysis I provide. But I am not willing to acknowledge that, simply because others do not share my Christian convictions, they thereby represent a more general, practical, or realistic morality. Indeed I mean to challenge those who do not share my Christian presuppositions by asking how they think war became or continues to be susceptible to moral analysis. For after all, Christians created just war reflection because of their nonviolent convictions; they assumed that those who would use violence bore the burden of proof for doing so. Thus the wide reach of pacifism becomes clear, for if you do not believe nonviolence is normative, then why assume that war needs justification and/or control?

For by contrast to just war theory, there are accounts of war that free us from such restraint and judgment. Though there are many different forms of political realism, in general political realists assume that war is neither good nor bad but simply a necessary part of human life, given the violent tendencies of "human nature" as displayed particularly in relations between groups. In such a view, war should not be actively sought, but at times it may be necessary given the lack of any means short of war for resolving international disputes.

It is my contention that the Gulf War was conceived and fought by such political realists, who found it useful to justify it on just war grounds; the result resembled an old-fashioned crusade. No doubt some have gone about this justification cynically, but I suspect that many realists who have justified the war on just war grounds genuinely believe the war was conceived and fought as a just war. But from a realist perspective, with its relative absence of moral strictures, what must be acknowledged is that those with the biggest armies and the best technology can call any war they have won just if they so choose.

The Gulf War was a sobering episode for many of us who have argued for the importance of disciplining American reflection and practice of war on just war grounds. Even though I am a pacifist, I have maintained that it would be a great good if moral reflection by Americans concerning war could be formed by just war considerations. But that possibility seems more remote now. What has often been observed is as pertinent today as at any time in the past: Americans prefer to go to war only if the war is a crusade—that is, a war whose cause is so noble that the standard moral and political limits are set aside in the service of a vastly greater good. Thus Americans always want to fight wars to defend such abstract concepts as freedom and democracy, or, in special fits of hubris, to fight wars to end all wars.

Those who think that wars should be governed by a nation-state's political interests—that is, realists—and those who are advocates of just war share in common a distaste for a crusade justification of war. The realists regret it because often the ideological justifications given for a war make it difficult to end the war when our interests have been achieved. An example for realists is the irrational prolonging of World War II by forcing Germany to accept "unconditional surrender." Just warriors abjure the crusade because the "good cause" often overrides the limited moral purpose that originally justified the war as well as often shoulders aside the principle of noncombatant immunity.

But in the Gulf War, both these accounts of war tended to be submerged by the American penchant to fight a "good war." The realist account of the war was subtly shifted into a crusade mode by borrowing tenets of just war theory. So just war thinking proved powerless to rein in the grand ambitions of a realist war fought primarily to "make Americans feel good about themselves after Vietnam." And thus, surprisingly, it may be that pacifists are better served by a realist account of war—a war fought for strict self-interest and little moral pretention—than by wars of massively powerful nations cloaked in the universal pretentions of "the just war theory." Of course, such universalism is what we expect from imperial nations, since their power protects them from recognizing they are serving their own interests. Thus the Gulf War was claimed to be necessary in order to oppose aggression, but it actually served the American interest of building a "new world order."

In this respect it is worth considering the recent history of how just war theory became a prominent discourse among mainstream Protestants. Recoiling from what they perceived to be the failure of the idealist aims of World War I, American Protestants took a more or less pacifist stance against war following the armistice of 1918. Their "pacifism" was "liberal," as it drew on humanistic presumptions that the human race had outgrown war as a method of resolving disputes. In other words, they thought the problem with war was not that it offended the God revealed in Christ but that war was irrational given the progress of the human race. In an interesting way this kind of "pacifism" was the mirror image of a crusade justification of war—if wars could not accomplish great goods then they should not take place.

This vague but quite influential pacifism was powerfully attacked by Reinhold Niebuhr during his tenure as Professor of Applied Christianity at Union Theological Seminary in New York. In the process of writing classics such as *Moral Man and Immoral Society,* Niebuhr became the most, and perhaps the last, influential Protestant public theologian in America. He achieved this status, however, exactly because he provided the theological justification to support the liberal ideology of the rising political elite, whose self-interest was commensurate with making America a world power.

Niebuhr subjected liberal pacifism, based as it was on progressivist views of history, to a withering critique because of its failure to acknowledge the sinful character of human existence. It was Niebuhr who prepared American Christians to acknowledge that war is an evil, but a necessary evil that we should accept, if we are to be serious about achieving relative justice within this world—which is all the justice we should hope for in this life. Niebuhr argued that there is no alternative to a world constituted by nation-state systems and, accordingly, that war is a necessary constituent of that system. Thus "peace" for Niebuhr can never mean an attempt to rid the world of war; rather, "peace" is a word for "order," and that order too often serves the interests of status quo powers. If you are for justice, therefore, you cannot exclude the use of violence and war. In effect Niebuhr gave a theological justification for political realism.

It was a great project of Paul Ramsey, Professor of Theological Ethics at Princeton University and author of *War and the Christian Conscience,* to accept the fundamental presuppositions of Niebuhr's account of politics and war but to discipline it by just war reflection. Ramsey saw clearly that Niebuhr's account lacked the kind of discriminating criteria that would allow Christians to discern when a war was legitimate as well as how it should be fought. Ramsey argued that just war reflection is a necessary constituent of Western civilization's Christian presuppositions, which are especially exemplified in matters of war and peace by the commitment to protect the innocent neighbor—thus the importance for Ramsey, in contrast to Niebuhr, of the protection of noncombatants.

Accordingly, Ramsey thought he was able to defend just war as a coherent theory in practice because of the presumption that we live in a Christian civilization. He did not assume that those who accepted just war in fact were Christians, but he did think they continued to share the habits and moral presuppositions that Christianity had instilled within the social milieu of the West. Not the least of those presumptions was that the American social order was built on the conviction that we would rather die as individuals, and even as a whole people, than directly kill one innocent human being. For Ramsey, that meant war must be pursued in a manner that may require more people to die in order to avoid directly attacking noncombatants—the innocent neighbors of any war.

For example, in Ramsey's account of just war, dropping the atomic bomb on Hiroshima and Nagasaki was profoundly immoral. It would have been better for more Japanese and American soldiers to die on the beaches of Japan than for noncombatants to be killed at Hiroshima and Nagasaki. Such judgments are necessary if Ramsey is right that intrinsic to the practice of just war is the protection of noncombatants from direct attack. For Ramsey such judgments are a morally necessary condition to distinguish the killing done in war from murder.

Just war thinking, at least in theory, presumes therefore that there are some things one cannot do in order to win a war. War undertaken on just war grounds requires those who prosecute it to consider the possibility of surrender rather than to fight a war unjustly. It is such requirements which give rise to the tension between those who would think of war in just war categories and those who accept the more realist account of war. Ramsey attempted to wed the just war criteria to Niebuhr's essentially realist account of nation-state relations; I fear that the Gulf War has revealed it to be an unstable marriage indeed.

The example of Hiroshima and Nagasaki reminds us how difficult it is to think about war in the American context in a morally disciplined fashion. In many respects World War II continues to set a terrible precedent for American thinking about war. For that war is what most Americans think a just war is about—namely, a war you can fight to win using any means necessary because your cause is entirely just. Thus we want to fight wars which have, either explicitly or implicitly, the condition of unconditional surrender because we believe we are confronting a thoroughly corrupt and evil enemy.

Reinhold Niebuhr's realism was meant to chasten such views, since to fight a war for unconditional surrender means you are not prepared to fight for the kinds of limited purposes that wars should serve, given the political realities of the world. Just war advocates such as Ramsey also challenged the endemic crusade mentality of America, since at the heart of just war reflection is the assumption that wars have only limited political purposes in response to clear cases of injustice. That is why it is so important on just war grounds that wars be declared, since the enemy must clearly understand what surrender means so that the war does not become more violent than necessary. In contrast to the popular conception of a "good war," both realists and just war advocates share in common the attempt to make war serve limited political purposes.

Of course Vietnam proved to be a disastrous moral experience for Americans in this respect. The policymakers who gave us that war may have been realists, but they justified it as a crusade—a last-stand defense of freedom and democracy. As a result, it proved impossible to prosecute that war with proportionate force—that is, to use only the means necessary to accomplish the end of the war. Exactly because the war had to be described as a defense of freedom and democracy, the means used in the war became disproportionate to what either a realist or a just warrior would have conceived as its more limited purposes. After Vietnam, Americans desperately needed to fight a "good war"—that is, a war that could restore the American belief that we only fight wars when the cause is unambiguously good.

An essential episode in this recent history of just war thinking is the conflict we have had with the Soviet Union called "the Cold War." That war was fought on crusade grounds in which complete good was opposed to complete evil. One need not give more credence than is due to Ronald Reagan's presumptions of the "evil empire" to nonetheless realize that U.S. foreign and military policy since World War II has essentially not been determined by just war presuppositions. American nuclear targeting policies, which would lead to massive civilian death tolls, are an obvious problem for just war reflection, as Paul Ramsey rightly saw. Also problematic for just war thinking has been the overwhelming fact that America's military forces have been organized to fight a massive and technologically sophisticated war against another world power that has sought, like the United States, to expand its influence as widely as possible.

Which brings us to the Gulf War and the attempt to justify that war in just war terms. The war in the Gulf was prosecuted by a military that was shaped by realist presuppositions, justified by the crusade rhetoric of the Cold War, and determined not to repeat Vietnam. Americans were able to fight the war in the Gulf as an allegedly just war, not because America is a nation whose foreign and military policies are formed by just war doctrine, but because America is a nation whose military has been shaped by realists to serve the crusade against communism. American Christians, undisciplined as they are by any serious reflection on the morality of war, enthusiastically backed this war as a providential instance of good versus evil.

Against the background of this history, the use of the just war criteria by President Bush almost appears comedic. He used the criteria as if they had dropped from heaven. Questions about who is using the criteria, to what purpose, and when were simply ignored. Just war theory appears as a kind of law—the only issue seems to be whether the law has been "broken." I am not surprised by this use: many have observed that in liberal societies such as America, it is almost inevitable that the law becomes our morality—witness, for example, the current enthusiasm for "ethical" behavior by those in Congress or involved in business. By "ethical" they mean they have broken no law.

Such use of just war theory to "justify" the Gulf War is not unlike schoolyard morality. Children often assume that questions of right or wrong primarily turn on whether a rule has been broken. In like manner the only question about the Gulf War is whether it met all the conditions of just war. To begin to evaluate the war on such grounds is to accept terms of analysis that are childish—that is, like children we are asked to begin thinking morally without any consideration for where our morality has come from.

When just war is construed in such an abstract way, we forget the social, political, and economic considerations that are necessary for the serious use of the theory. It is no wonder that the Administration found it useful to make just war criteria appear as if they are generally agreed-upon presuppositions that can be used by any right-thinking people. Those who possess hegemonic power always claim to represent a universal morality. Such universal claims are meant to create a social and historical amnesia that is intended to make us forget how the dominant achieved power in the first place.

For example, consider this seemingly innocent paragraph from Richard John Neuhaus's article in the *Wall Street Journal* (January 29, 1991), entitled "Just War and This War." Neuhaus notes that "just war theory was formulated by Augustine [died 430], refined by Thomas Aquinas [died 1274] and Francisco de Vitori [died 1546], and developed in more or less its present form by Hugo Grotius [died 1645], who was often called the father of international law. Skeptics claim that just war theory is useless because it has not stopped wars. That is like saying the Ten Commandments should be discarded because they have not eliminated theft, lying, and adultery. The presumption of just war theory is against the use of military force. The theory erects an obstacle course of moral testing aimed at preventing the unjust resort to war."

The kind of history Neuhaus provides of the settings of just war theory creates the illusion that the just war criteria have been unchanging through the centuries. Why the criteria were produced and reproduced, and their various statuses and emphases, seem irrelevant for assessing the theory's validity. For example, the fact that just war reflection in the Middle Ages was predominantly used to help confessors discipline Christians who participated in war is obviously quite different from the use of just war reflection by the princes of the Holy Roman Empire, who employed it in their many wars of expansion. And furthermore, there is a vast difference between the application of such thinking in the Middle Ages and the application of just war theory in the developing nation-state system to which Grotius was responding; in this latter system the theory served not Christian princes but secular politicians. Neuhaus and others seem to believe that such historical and political considerations are irrelevant to the theory's meaning for today.

John Howard Yoder, the Mennonite theologian, has pointed out many of the problems implicit in such an ahistorical appropriation of the tradition. For instance, he has noted that just war thinking was not intended for use in democracies. Thus when the just war tradition said that the decisions to go to war belong to the sovereigns they did not mean the democratic sovereign, but rather the king or the prince primarily within the Holy Roman Empire ("Just War Tradition: Is It Credible?" *The Christian Century* [March 13, 1991], 295–98). Yoder continues, "The democratic vision which makes decisions that are 'sovereign' changes how the system has to work. Disinformation and spin control invalidate the administrator's claim to legitimacy. Civilian and military administrators are not trained to distinguish dissent from disloyalty, secrecy from security. They thus can refuse to provide 'the people' with the wherewithal for evaluating the claimed justifications."

In the case of the Gulf War, the moral problems arising from such disinformation have become clear. The way the Administration and military have controlled the descriptions of the war, Americans now believe that they have prosecuted a war in which "no one got killed." The fact that there are thousands of Iraqi casualties is not thought to be morally relevant. As a result the Iraqi war has put the realist and the just warrior alike in the difficult position of having to meet the unreal expectations of the public in the future. Now they must justify future wars to the American people who believe in the technological fantasy of a war in which no one gets killed—when "no one" means any of "our" soldiers. As a result of this spin control, which has fired the crusade mentality, the fundamental question for advocates of just war theory or realism is how democracies are to develop virtues in their citizens in order to fight wars with limited purposes, not crusades.

The abstract presentation of just war criteria, as given by Neuhaus, also ignores when and how decisions to go to war are made. Again Yoder points to the hidden problems in the use of the just war tradition. The just war paradigm for decisions about war, he notes, assumes a punctual conception of legal and moral decision making. "What is either right or wrong is that punctual decision, based upon the facts of the case at just that instant, and the just war tradition delivers the criteria for adjudicating that decision. This procedure undervalues the longitudinal dimensions of the conflict" (Ibid.). In other words, what such a view of moral decision fails to see is that most of the important decisions are already well in place prior to the decision to initiate the actual conflict. For example, it is now clear that the decision to go to war—on a massive scale in the Gulf—was made long before most Americans knew about it.

Oddly enough, those who use the just war criteria as a set of general rules look very much like situation ethicists. Such ethicists often presented moral dilemmas as if they were simply givens that could be dealt with in the same way from any point of view (like mud puddles that you either have to step over, wade through, or go around). Situationalists thrived on examples that poked holes in the general "in principle" prohibitions against suicide, adultery, and killing by suggesting that at certain times the doing of such actions would produce the greatest good. Their examples had power exactly because they were divorced from any thick descriptions of actual people and the histories that had brought them to such contexts—for example, in order to save ten people in a cave, can you dynamite the one stuck in the cave opening?

In like manner we are asked by Neuhaus and others to decide whether the prosecution of the war in the Gulf was in accordance with the "just war theory." But that question assumes there is a simple yes or no answer; also, the question makes it appear that the options before American foreign policy were only to go to war or to refrain from war. By framing the question in this way, we are led away from the prior ethical task of analyzing the policy presumptions which made such a war seem so necessary and inevitable in the first place. For example, much is made of congressional approval of the Administration's decision to prosecute the war in the Gulf, the implication being that the Administration went well beyond the just war requirement that the war should be declared by legitimate authority. The fact that the Administration had already put hundreds of thousands of troops in Saudi Arabia prior to the congressional debate is somehow not thought to have significantly prejudiced that decisive vote.

Furthermore, as has often been pointed out, the Administration's supportive relationship with Iraq, and in particular Saddam Hussein, prior to his invasion of Kuwait must be seen as bearing some responsibility for the tragic events that followed. On good realist geopolitical grounds, the United States may have been prudent in its policy to support Saddam Hussein as a counterbalance to Iran in the area, but such support obviously led Hussein to believe that he could pursue certain foreign policy initiatives that the United States had no reason to oppose on self-interested or moral grounds. How could he have known, given the Administration's prior realist support, that America was so serious about being a just war nation?

The purported justifications for going to war have also largely been discussed in an abstract fashion that denies many relevant, concrete questions. For example, the general presumption that the United States had to intervene because America is morally obligated to resist aggression wherever and whenever it occurs is at best an exaggeration and at worst a lie. It is clear that American foreign policy does not obligate the United States to intervene anytime there seems to be an unjust aggression. The United States did not militarily intervene when China invaded Tibet, or when Russia invaded Afghanistan, or when Indonesia invaded Timor. What made this aggression so peculiarly an affront to justice that it made our intervention necessary?

Indeed, a clear view of the entire war reveals a bewildering mix of realist politics, crusade appeals, and just war pronouncements. For instance, President Bush's description of Saddam Hussein as a Hitler is particularly perverse given the President's avowed commitment to just war doctrine, which should abjure such hyped descriptions of a foe. There is no question that this was a carefully calculated move by the Administration—a move that invited the American people to think about the war in terms antithetical to just war aims. If you are confronting a Hitler, then your crusading aim must be to remove that which is thoroughly evil. Ironically, though, the Administration can claim that in spite of the description of Saddam Hussein as Hitler, it prosecuted the war justly. For the declared U.S. purpose was to liberate Kuwait, and once that had been accomplished, hostilities ceased. But the crucial question is whether that cessation was the result of just war considerations or realist questions of the policy toward other Arab countries. I do not mean to suggest that just war considerations and policy questions always are separable in principle, but I raise the question since it is by no means clear how they are interrelated in this instance. The Kurds seem clearly to have been sacrificed in the name of the U.S. interest to remain in good standing with Arab allies. In like manner, it is amazing to see how quickly Assad of Syria becomes a "statesman" when it is in the interest of American foreign policy.

Advocates of just war reasoning explain away the problems inherent in such a mishmash of ideas by arguing that we must distinguish between moral and prudential judgments. Such a distinction assumes that just war criteria are clear; the only question is how they are to be applied. Thus Richard Neuhaus, in his *Wall Street Journal* article, notes that while the criteria of justice are clear—last resort, probability of success, proportionate means, and so forth—they still depend on prudential judgments by political and military experts. Likewise Bryan Hehir, in his article "The Moral Calculus of War" *(Commonweal* [February 22, 1991], 126), argues that "the judgment about the last resort is by definition open to prudential calculations about what is possible, what is wise, and when have all efforts been exhausted." Michael Walzer employs the same distinction between morality and prudence in his article on the Gulf crisis in *The New Republic* (January 28, 1991, 14), where he notes, "We must ask whether there are any means short of war for defeating the aggressor and whether the defeat can be inflicted at costs proportional to the values under attack. Unfortunately, neither just war theory nor any other perspective of moral philosophy helps much in answering these questions. Political or military judgments are called for, and here theologians and philosophers have no special expertise. War as a 'last resort' is an endlessly receding possibility, invoked mostly by people who prefer never to resist aggression with force. After all, there is always something else to do, another diplomatic note, another meeting."

This distinction between morality and prudence looks innocent enough, but it is exactly the source of the fundamental difficulty in the use of just war theory in the Gulf War. The distinction derived from accounts of morality that assume "the moral" can be determined in a manner that is abstracted from concrete communities and corresponding practices—that is, the widespread modern belief that morality is a distinct realm distinguishable from religious convictions, social practices, manners, and so on. Moral principles presumably can be and indeed must be justified in abstract and historical arguments: What is right or wrong is right or wrong for all times and places. Such an account of morality creates the peculiar modern presumption that we must first conceive and justify something called "morality" and then ask how to apply it. Hence the recent enthusiasm for "applied ethics" concerning matters of medicine, business, and law, as if ethics is derived from philosophical speculation in the same way that engineering is derived from theoretical physics (a terrible analogy if you know anything about physics and/or engineering). But when you have an ethic which is so abstract that you have to ask how it is to be applied, then you know you have an ideology.

It is of course this paradigm of moral rationality that I have tried to counter at the beginning of this essay by the declaration that I am a pacifist writing as a Christian. I do not pretend I can write about the war for anyone anywhere anytime, as if such a position would ensure "objectivity." Such an "objective" point of view is but a form of the mental imperialism that produced the presumption that Americans "had" to intervene in the Gulf: There an imperial power pursued a war on the specious presumption that all right-thinking people could not help but agree that the "facts" required a moral response that "unfortunately" meant war.

The distinction between morality and prudence is so inscribed into the self-interest of imperial powers that I do not presume it can be defeated by argument. Rev. Michael Baxter C.S.C. has at least suggested to me an interesting test for those who assume the distinction is intelligible for assessing the Gulf War on just war grounds. They should ask themselves what they might possibly learn about how the war was conducted that might make them change their minds and deem the Gulf War unjust. If, for example, the United States' primary object was to make Iraq withdraw from Kuwait, then was the bombing policy pursued in Iraq itself just? Why was it necessary at the same time the United States pursued the war in Kuwait to also try to eliminate Saddam Hussein's nuclear capacity? Surely the potential to make nuclear weapons is not itself unjust, as otherwise the American policy in that regard would be problematic. The implications of American bombing policy in Iraq, moreover, surely must raise questions about the principle of discrimination, since such policy was clearly meant to disrupt the social infrastructure of Iraq. And if any of these considerations lead just war theorists to conclude that the Gulf War was (at least in part) unjust, then there is a further question to face: what will the United States do to make reparation for those parts of the war which, in hindsight, were morally unjust?

The distinction between morality and prudence is invoked by many Christians who justify the Gulf War on just war grounds because it lets them avoid "the more." Their appeals to prudence excuse them from naming what difference it might make that they are Christians for how they think about this war. For example, Professor Stephen Fowl of Loyola College, Baltimore, observes that, in terms of the criterion of last resort, Richard Neuhaus

> rightly notes that any judgment that all previous options have been exhausted is a prudential one; it is a judgment call for which one must take responsibility. What he fails to mention, however, is despite the contingencies of any particular situation, what counts as a last resort is going to be different for those who are also committed to loving their enemies than for those who are committed to maintaining a certain standard of living for themselves. If Christians are to reason both prudentially and faithfully, they will need to understand that criteria for determining the justice of any particular war are deeply tied to their convictions about God, the cross, their neighbors and their enemy—convictions which many others employing the language of just war theories do not share ("On the Frustration of Practical Reasoning," unpublished paper, 4–5).

By challenging the distinction between morality and prudence, I am not calling into question the need of practical wisdom for moral guidance. But as Aristotle and Thomas Aquinas emphasized, only the person of virtue has the capacity for such wisdom. For prudence is not the application of moral principles to concrete problems—an abstract project of the intellect done best by so-called experts. Rather, prudence is discernment arising from good character—a process inseparable from the virtue of those doing the discerning. Furthermore, what is discerned—indeed, all that can be discerned—are the courses of action that matter because of the virtue of those discerning. Thus are principles useless when they are not constituted in the practices of virtue that form and are formed by good people. Thus, too, are judgments of practical wisdom necessarily different for Christians, a community which ought especially to be formed by the virtues of faith, hope, and love.

If Christians can ever be just warriors, they can be so only with profound sadness. As just warriors they can never kill gladly. Indeed, if Paul Ramsey was right in his defense of just war, the Christian soldier should not intend to kill the enemy but rather seek only to incapacitate him so as to prevent him from achieving his purpose. In fact, the Christian soldier would rather die, or at least take greater risks, than kill unnecessarily. These thoughts should, from a Christian perspective, make the Gulf War even more doubtful, since there is every reason to believe that the U.S. strategy was to inflict intense destruction on the enemy by using means that would not risk American lives; furthermore, this was done in order to avoid adverse domestic political consequences.

Surely the saddest aspect of the war for Christians should have been its celebration as a victory and its treatment of its warriors as heroes. No doubt many fought bravely and even heroically, but the orgy of crusading patriotism that this war unleashed should surely have been resisted by Christians. The flags and yellow ribbons on churches are testimony to how little Christians in America realize that our loyalty to God is incompatible with those who would war in the name of an abstract justice. Christians should have recognized that such "justice" is but another form of idolatry to the degree it asked us to kill. I pray that God will judge us accordingly.

(I am indebted to Professor Greg Jones, Mr. David DeCosse, Mr. David Matzko, and Mr. Philip Kenneson for their critique of earlier drafts of this paper.)

APPENDIX ONE

Modern War and the Christian Conscience
La Civiltà Cattolica

TRANSLATED BY
PETER HEINEGG

Only a few months have passed since the war in the Gulf, which began on the night of January 16 and ended on February 28, 1991, yet almost no one talks about it anymore. A thick curtain of silence has descended on the war, as if we wanted to put it out of our minds as quickly and completely as possible. It's quite curious: At any other time under such circumstances, there would be a rush to discover and publicize what really happened, but today we still don't know what the Gulf War actually was. We don't know for sure, for example, the most essential fact: Exactly how many people, both soldiers and civilians, died on the Iraqi side? Why does no one, on either side, let the word out? (There must be *somebody* who knows.) Perhaps governments are silent because the war was a tremendous, pointless slaughter, and it's politically—if not morally—advantageous for people not to realize this. In any event, the war in the Gulf has once again, and in the most dramatic fashion, brought the Christian conscience face to face with the problem of modern warfare.

Why do we speak of "modern war," and not just "war"? Because modern war is a radically different reality from the wars of the past, and because the theoretical categories and moral judgments once applied to past wars no longer seem applicable here. At bottom, to be sure, war remains the same: a lethal contest, fed by hatred, in which physical violence is unleashed in all its brutality; a duel that aims at "crushing" (von Clausewitz) or "destroying" (Mao Zedong) the enemy. Clausewitz writes:

> War is simply a duel on a larger scale . . . Each one tries, through his physical force, to subject the other to his will. His immediate plan is to strike down the adversary so as to render him incapable of further resistance. War, therefore, is an act of violence designed to force the adversary to carry out our will. Violence, in order to meet violence, arms itself with the inventions of the arts and sciences. It is accompanied by slight restrictions, scarcely worth mentioning, which it imposes on itself in the name of international law, but which in reality do not weaken its force. Violence, that is, physical violence . . . is thus the means; the end is to impose our will on the enemy. To achieve this end in all security it is necessary to disarm the enemy *(Vom Kriege [On War]* [Leipzig: Insel, 1944], 59–60).

War, then, is always an evil. But its wickedness becomes increasingly evident the closer we get to modern war. For some thinkers, the wars of the past could be justified by the relatively limited damage they inflicted, but this can't be done with modern war. How did the transition to modern war take place? Von Clausewitz recalls that while it always remains violence, war "arms itself with the inventions of the arts and sciences." Hence it gradually changes as weapons are perfected—that is, are made more destructive and murderous—with the help of scientific inventions. Thus the introduction of gunpowder brought about the first great revolution in the art of war; and with the perfecting of firearms, war became more homicidal.

With the introduction of air power, which could cause damage all across a country, of submarines, which could hit mercantile and military vessels wherever they might be, of long-range weapons, which could strike from a great distance, and of tanks, which made deep and rapid inroads into lines of defense, war once again underwent a profound change. Now the entire country and the whole population were caught up in wars. *Any* group of combatants or noncombatants could be attacked, either because the population was located near military targets, because the strategy was to break down the morale of the enemy nation with carpet bombing, because it wasn't always possible to distinguish between "military" and "civilian" targets, or, finally, because even strictly civilian targets could be considered military ones insofar as they served to fuel the enemy's resistance and its war-making capacity.

In this way war, hitherto "local" and "partial," becomes ever more "total" in a triple sense: primarily, because it involves the whole territory, the entire population, all the cultural, artistic, and religious goods, and all the economic riches of a country; secondly, because it involves not just two countries or a group of countries but many countries and has a tendency to involve the whole world; finally, because of the recourse to weapons of total and indiscriminate destruction. The first example of total war was World War I, but not until World War II do we see a full-blown total war. Not only did World War II involve practically all the peoples of the world, not only did it lead to the destruction of entire nations and to the physical elimination of millions of persons, but it brought into use weapons of mass destruction —both with the practice of carpet bombing, which aimed at leveling and destroying entire cities (as happened with Dresden on February 13–14, 1944) and, above all, with the dropping of two atomic bombs, on Hiroshima (August 6, 1945) and Nagasaki (August 9, 1945).

The truth is that on August 6, 1945, the human race entered a new phase in its history, one radically different from all that went before: the age of total war. From 1945 to today, with the enormous development of nuclear, biological, and chemical weapons, this term has taken on a much more sinister meaning than in the past. The Second World War *was* a total war, with its funeral procession of over 50 million people—most of them civilians—and its enormous destruction of every sort of property. But a war fought today with nuclear weapons would be far more "total," because in its first hours it would cause hundreds of millions of deaths and would mean the destruction of every form of life on a large portion of the planet.

But even when nuclear or chemical weapons are not used, modern war is still total, though in a different way. The war in the Gulf is a clear instance of this. No nuclear weapons were fired, although some thought was given to the use of "tactical" nuclear weapons, and it was feared that Iraq might employ chemical weapons. But the weapons that were used were terrible and destructive enough to cause the death—according to unofficial but reliable sources—of 175,000 Iraqi soldiers and 30,000 civilians, as well as the practically complete destruction of the country's infrastructure (roads, bridges, irrigation systems, and so forth) and of its industrial and economic fabric (one United Nations envoy said Iraq had been blasted back to the "preindustrial era"). Thus we are in the presence of a radical shift in the

110

very nature of war; modern war is something fundamentally different from past wars. This fact—as *Gaudium et spes* (n. 80) justly notes—"obliges us to consider arguments for war from a completely new perspective *(mente omnino nova)."*

What is the "completely new perspective" the Council speaks of? For the Christian conscience, it evidently means confronting the problem of war in a radically different manner. With this in mind it will be useful to know how the Church viewed this problem in the past. In making a thumbnail sketch of the history of the Church's approach to war, we will distinguish the practical stance that the Church has taken toward war down through the ages from the doctrinal system that Catholic theologians, philosophers, and canon lawyers have tried to elaborate—without much success, but with the laudable intention of circumscribing and regulating the phenomenon of war.

As for practical behavior, it has varied with historical periods. During the persecutions (first to fourth century), the prevalent attitude was opposition to war and military service. In *Contra Celsum* V, 33, Origen writes, "We do not brandish the sword against any people, nor do we learn to make war, because we have become children of peace through Jesus, whom we follow as our leader." Nevertheless, there were Christians in the imperial army who thought their faith was in no way incompatible with military service. Some churchmen were more easygoing on this score, while others were harsher. For example, Hippolytus of Rome (ca. 170–235 C.E.) puts the Church's position this way: "The subordinate soldier shall not kill anyone. If he receives the order to do so, he must not carry it out; and he shall not take the oath. If he refuses, let him be excommunicated *(reiciatur).* The catechumens or faithful who wish to become soldiers will be excommunicated because they have despised God" *(The Apostolic Tradition,* 16).

In the fourth and fifth centuries, with the Christianization of the Roman empire, a profound change occurred in the Church's attitude toward the army and military service. Under Theodosius II's law of December 7, 415, Christians were obliged, under pain of excommunication, to do military service. Pagans were forbidden to join the army, which was thus made up exclusively of Catholics. This change can be explained by the fact that, in the eyes of Christians who had emerged from Diocletian's tremendous persecution, the Christian empire seemed to be the realization of the messianic kingdom, and the Christian emperor the vicegerent of Christ—hence his wars were necessarily "holy" and oriented toward salvation. Besides, in the north and east the invasions of the "barbarians," the pagans, and Arian heretics such as the Goths had already begun. The Catholic empire was in danger (in 410 came the terrible trauma of Alaric's conquest of Rome), and Catholics felt impelled to fight to defend it. So the Church accepted the army and war, though only as a sad "necessity" owing to the "iniquity of the unjust," because "waging war seems happiness to the wicked, but for the good it is a necessity *(belligerare malis videtur felicitas, bonis necessitas)"* (St. Augustine, *The City of God* IV, 15).

Both before and during the Middle Ages the Church's attitude changed again. On the one hand, in a society that had now become a single great *Respublica Christiana,* the Church declared its opposition to the wars that Christian princes and states fought among themselves. Nicholas I (died 867) denounced war as "always Satanic in its origin," and the Council of Narbonne, (1045) affirmed that "a Christian who kills another Christian spills the blood of Christ."

For this reason the Church sought to prevent wars between Christians, offering to arbitrate disputes—an effort successfully undertaken by Paschal II, Gregory VII, and Innocent III, the last of whom solemnly stated that the Pope was the sovereign mediator on earth. Above all, the Church tried to limit the times of fighting by imposing the "truce of God," that is, a ban against fighting on certain days of the week (from Wednesday to Monday morning), in some seasons of the year (from Advent to Epiphany and from Ash Wednesday to the octave of Easter), and on the feast days of the Lord, the Virgin Mary, the Apostles, St. Lawrence, St. Michael, and the principal patron saints, along with fast days and vigils (cf. the *Decretal* of Gregory IX, book 1, tit. XXXIV, *On the Truce and Peace*). In addition, the Church laid down norms for the protection of persons not involved in a given war and the inviolability of places functioning as asylums for noncombatants. The Church, in fact, considered that its peculiar "ministry" (Gregory IV) was to preserve the peace between citizens.

On the other hand, the Church maintained that a war fought "against the enemies of the faith" was not only just but meritorious. Hence the Church could oblige believers to go on crusade, which it considered "an affair of Jesus Christ," for whose success all Christians had to collaborate. When a crusade began, Christian princes were required to stop warring on each other for four years and to join the crusade to "free the Holy Land from the hands of the impious" (Fourth Lateran Council, Const. 72, December 14, 1215).

During the wars of religion of the sixteenth and seventeenth centuries, the Church took the side of the Catholic states fighting against Protestant states and princes. But as political interests gradually prevailed over religious ones in the wars between European states, we can observe in the

Church's attitude a sort of detachment that increasingly tended to become outright opposition to war. Nevertheless, this rule was not made absolute until the twentieth-century papacy, from Benedict XV to John Paul II.

Turning now from practical behavior to look at the Catholic doctrinal position on the problem of war, we find that for many hundreds of years theologians have defended the theory of the "just war." While this notion never became official teaching, it was sanctioned by the Church's magisterium. It starts out from the assumption that war isn't always and intrinsically immoral, but may be necessary in certain cases. Thus there are "just wars" *(justa bella)* and "unjust wars." St. Augustine argues that a war is just if it is waged to avenge injustices *(ad ulciscendum iniurias)*—that is, to make up for the violation of a right. A war is unjust when waged out of "desire to do harm" *(nocendi cupiditas),* out of "lust for power" *(libido dominandi),* to "enlarge an empire" *(regni cupiditas),* or to obtain riches or glory. If fought for such reasons, war is "robbery on a grand scale *(grande latrocinium)" (The City of God* IV, 6).

Augustine's teaching on the "just war" became part of the patrimony of medieval theology, which went on defining the conditions for such wars with greater precision. Thus Gratian in his *Decretum* (p. II, c. XXIII, q. 2, c. 1) specified the causes that made a war "just": It had to be declared by a competent authority *(ex edicto geritur),* and it had to be waged to recover one's own property *(de rebus repetendis)* or to repel aggression by an enemy *(propulsandorum hostium causa).* In his turn, St. Thomas stressed that three things were needed for a war to be just: (1) the authority of the prince *(auctoritas principis),* because it is the prince's task to defend the state from both internal disturbances and external enemies; (2) a just cause *(causa justa),* which consists in the fact that those being fought deserve to be fought because of some wrong they have done *(propter aliquam culpam);* and (3) a proper intention on the part of the ones fighting the war *(intentio bellantium recta),* namely to promote good or avoid evil. Even if there was a just cause for fighting the war, without a correct intention—that is, if the war was waged out of a desire to hurt the adversary, out of lust for power or greed for riches, or cruelly and in a spirit of vengeance *(ulciscendi crudelitas)*—the war would not be allowed *(Summa theol.* II-II, q. 40, a. 1, c). The sign of a proper intention was the quest for peace, because "those who wage just wars seek peace" (ibid., ad 3).

The concept of the "just war" was taken up again by the theologians and canon lawyers of the sixteenth and seventeenth centuries (F. de Vitoria, F. Suárez, and L. Molina), but with one basic difference: The "just war" became the "right [to wage] war"—that is, we move from the "moral" plane *(bellum justum)* to the "legal" plane *(jus belli).* This change in approach can be explained by the fact that the later centuries of the Middle Ages saw the birth of nation-states or, rather, the "modern state," whose essential feature is "sovereignty." In other words, the modern state does not recognize any power higher than itself, and it believes itself to be the sole judge of its own interests and rights. If it feels that any of its rights have been violated by another state or thinks that it ought to enforce certain of its rights (which it alone may determine), it has the *ius belli.* This amounts to the "right" to wage war on another state, if it thinks that war is the best way to defend or vindicate its sovereign rights. Obviously this theory of the *ius belli* has to lead to permanent conflict among states. Catholic theologians and canon lawyers accept the principle of the "sovereignty" of the state and hence its "right to wage war," but they try to limit and restrain this right through the theory of the "just war."

According to de Vitoria, one has a right to wage war

when the war is just; and there are three purposes that make it just. The first is to defend one's possessions, to recover property unjustly taken away, and to repair the damage suffered. The second is to punish the guilty—that is, those who by violating the right of another have done some wrong deserving chastisement. But there must be a "certain, serious, and persistent" violation of a right. The third is to mount a legitimate defense against an unjust aggression, because "it is lawful to repel violence with violence *(vim vi repellere licet)*."

To these three causes that render a war just, de Vitoria adds two essential correctives. Above all, there has to be a fair proportion between the gravity of the injustice one has suffered (or is on the point of suffering) and the harm that will result from the war: "When great evils will be the consequence of a war, it cannot be just" *(De iure belli,* 33 [Lyons: J. Boyer, 1557], 405). Secondly, "if a war is useful for a province or a state, but does harm to the whole world or to Christendom, then that war becomes unjust" *(De potestate civili,* 13, op. cit., 193). This approach to the "just war" became the classic theory of Catholic theology and may be found in traditional manuals of ethics and moral theology.

What can be said about this theory? To begin with, we must recognize that it had no intention of "justifying" war, but rather of limiting its frequency and ferocity by assigning extremely precise and severe conditions to be met before a war could be called "just." Thus the intention of Catholic theologians and canon lawyers in working out the theory of the "just war" was a praiseworthy one. A war waged for a just motive was not allowed to cause "great evils" or "harm to the whole world," or else it would become "unjust." It was not supposed to be waged with ferocity nor to inflict on the enemy more damage than required to obtain the ends for which it was being fought. But these conditions were and are impossible to abide by; because of its very nature, war is waged with brutality. It always causes greater harm than the advantages that can be derived from it in terms of justice and right. And it tends to inflict on the enemy considerably more damage than needed to achieve the end for which a just war is fought. What motivates the ferocity peculiar to war is the wish not simply to reach the goal for which it was declared but to destroy the enemy so that he can never recover and become a future danger.

This explains the course of the war in the Gulf. It was waged for a "just" cause—the liberation of Kuwait from the Iraqi invasion. But by its own inexorable logic it led, first of all, to the systematic destruction of Iraq. We are told that ninety thousand tons of bombs were dropped, leaving an incalculable number of civilian dead and wounded. And then the war led to the destruction of the Iraqi army, so as to prevent Iraq from constituting a military danger in the future. Thus the liberation of Kuwait was purchased at the price of destroying a country and killing hundreds of thousands of people. At this point, can we still talk about a "just war"? Shouldn't we say instead that "just wars" can't exist because even when just causes come into play, the harm wars do by their very nature is so grave and horrendous that they can never be justified in the forum of conscience? This is all the more true because wars are not necessary and inevitable, since the injustices for which they are supposed to provide the remedy can be cured by other and no less effective means.

It is not true, as a matter of fact, that war is the *extrema ratio* (ultimate recourse or remedy), because there are always peaceful mechanisms for settling conflicts, so long as one has the will and the patience to make use of them. The declaration that war is the *extrema ratio* is often really an attempt to justify one's own wish to make war. But the most serious problem with the theory of the "just war" is that

117

most of the time the "just cause" serves as a legal and moral pretext for a war meant to be waged for reasons far different from the official ones.

Thus the theory of the "just war" is indefensible and has been abandoned. In reality—with the sole exception of a purely defensive war against acts of aggression—we can say that there are no "just wars," and there is no "right" to wage war. The "right of legitimate defense" is admitted by both Pius XII and Vatican II, at least in certain circumstances, when there is no international authority capable of resolving conflicts peacefully: "Since human freedom is able to touch off an unjust conflict hurtful to a nation, it is certain that such a nation can, under certain conditions, rise up in arms and defend itself" (Pius XII, *Discorsi e radiomessaggi,* Vol. XX [Rome: Polyglot Vatican Press, 1959], 173). For its part, the Council affirms that "war has unfortunately not been eradicated from the human condition. And so long as the danger of war exists and there is no competent international authority equipped with adequate forces, once all the possibilities of mutual accommodation have been exhausted, governments cannot be denied the right of legitimate self-defense *(ius legitimae defensionis)*" *(Gaudium et spes,* n. 79).

It must be stressed, however, that the war of legitimate self-defense becomes illegitimate "when the harm it does is not comparable with that caused by the injustice being suffered": if such is the case, "one can be obliged to suffer the injustice" (Pius XII, *Discorsi e radiomessaggi,* Vol. XV [Rome: Polyglot Vatican Press, 1954], 422). Furthermore, even in a war of legitimate self-defense, one may not employ weapons of total destruction and, above all, weapons liable to get out of control, whose use cannot be limited to the strict requirements of self-defense. Use of such weapons must be rejected as immoral, because "in this case one would no longer be dealing with 'defense' against injustice, or with a necessary 'safeguard' for legitimate possessions, but with the annihilation pure and simple of all human life within the war zone. This is not permitted for any reason whatsoever" (Pius XII, *Discorsi e radiomessaggi,* Vol. XVI [Rome: Polyglot Vatican Press, 1955], 169).

The theory of the "just war" (and even the war of legitimate self-defense, as Pius XII notes) was plunged into a terminal crisis by the advent of modern warfare, which by its very nature involves uncontrollable weapons of mass destruction. The wars of the past were fought with weapons that caused limited damage and were subject to control. By contrast, in modern war, armies fight with uncontrollable weapons of mass destruction, so that both soldiers and civilians are killed and wounded. This makes all talk of "surgical strikes" illusory. Both military targets and purely civilian targets are destroyed (because even when there is no desire to strike civilian populations, there is always the intent to demoralize the enemy).

In addition, the damage done by modern war cannot be limited, since it involves the practically complete destruction of a country. It can also cause enormous massacres of civilians: think of the destruction of Hamburg and Dresden by conventional bombs, and of Hiroshima and Nagasaki by atomic bombs, considered necessary to break an enemy who had indeed started the war by committing horrendous crimes. Modern war involves unleashing violence that, precisely because modern weapons are employed, becomes limitless.

The argument presented thus far also holds in the event that only conventional weapons are used. As we saw in the Gulf War, such weapons, thanks to technological innovations, have acquired an enormous destructive power: Recall the white phosphorus bombs reportedly used against the Iraqi soldiers fleeing Kuwait. But modern warfare involves the recourse to nuclear, chemical, and bacteriological weapons, and at the very least there is always the danger of such weapons being put to use. Vatican II affirms that "every act of war that aims indiscriminately at the destruction of entire cities or of vast regions and their inhabitants is a crime against God and against humanity itself *(est crimen contra Deum et ipsum hominem),* and must be firmly and un-hesitatingly condemned." Furthermore, "The characteristic danger of modern war *(belli hodierni)* consists in the fact that it offers those who possess the most modern weapons the opportunity to commit such crimes; and, by a certain inexorable linkage *(connexione quadam inexorabili),* it can prompt the will of human beings to make the most atrocious decisions" *(Gaudium et spes,* n. 80). Therefore, we must conclude that modern war is always immoral.

But, apart from being immoral, war today is useless and harmful. On the one hand, it doesn't resolve—except momentarily and speciously—the problems that triggered it. John XXIII argues in *Pacem in terris* (n. 127) that "in this age, which boasts of atomic power, it is senseless to think of war as a tool for redressing the violation of rights *(alienum est a ratione bellum iam aptum esse ad violata iura sarcienda)."* On the other hand, not only does war not re-solve problems, it aggravates them, making a solution im-possible. And it creates new and even more serious prob-lems: It lays the groundwork for future conflicts and wars, because the "peace" that wars end with is violently imposed on the losers by the winners, and hence such a truce gives rise in the vanquished to the desire for vengeance. And this itself becomes the seed of new wars. Thus the seed of World War II was the "peace" of Versailles, which ended World War I.

In reality, a war almost never ends with a true peace. It always leaves behind it a trail of hatred and the longing to get even—feelings that will explode the moment a suitable opportunity arises. War lights a fuse of hatred and violence that is extremely hard to extinguish.

War, therefore, is pointless because it doesn't solve problems; it is harmful because it aggravates the problems or makes them insoluble. Just how true this is can be seen, unfortunately, from the war in the Gulf. To be sure, Kuwait has been liberated, and the international rule of law restored—but at what cost and with what results? The cost has been the destruction of the invading country (Iraq) and the economic ruin of the country invaded (Kuwait). According to *The Economist,* the reconstruction of Kuwait will cost $100 billion. The war caused the slaughter of the Palestinians in Kuwait (and Iraqis too, of course) by Emir al-Sabah upon his return; it sparked the civil war in Iraq, with the massacre of Kurds and Shiites; and it led to the polluting of an immense area of the Persian Gulf—not to mention the gigantic military cost of the war, estimated by the Congressional Budget Office at around $190 billion.

On the other hand, now that the war in the Gulf is over, none of the most urgent problems of the Middle East—the plight of the Palestinians, the Lebanese, or the Kurds— seem to have found any easy or immediate solution. On the contrary, these and other problems born of the war have gotten worse, and their solution seems rather more doubtful. Thus it is evident that war is not only immoral, but irrational too, in its uselessness and the disasters that it unleashes.

This explains the position taken by the Church in the twentieth century with regard to war: it has absolutely condemned war and moved beyond the old arguments for the "just war" or "holy war" in defense of the faith. This attitude indicates an advance in Christian conscience regarding the absolute immorality of war. Thus the Church has formally condemned war in four important documents: the encyclical *Pacem Dei munus* by Benedict XV (May 23, 1920), the encyclical *Pacem in terris* by John XXIII (April 11, 1963), the pastoral constitution *Gaudium et spes* (December 7, 1965), and the encyclical *Centesimus annus* by John Paul II (May 1, 1991). To quote from this last: "No war ever again! War destroys the lives of the innocent; it teaches killing and throws even the lives of the killers into confusion. It leaves behind it a trail of rancor and hate, making it harder to achieve a just solution of the problems that provoked it. Just as within individual states the time has finally come when the system of private revenge and reprisals has been replaced by the rule of law, so it is urgent now that the same sort of progress take place in the international community" (n. 52). But at the very moment that it condemns war, the Church affirms that peace is possible. Peace "is not a dream, nor a utopia," and hence today we must "proceed resolutely toward the absolute proscription of war" (John Paul II). The human race is not condemned to the "fatality" of war, but can free itself from war's "necessity," or rather its slavery.

Then too the Church has an even more important and radical motive impelling it not just to condemn war but to promote peace. It must preach the Gospel, which is a "Gospel of peace," and so the proclamation and promotion of peace on earth are part of its religious mission. For this reason, when the Church speaks of the necessity of a commitment to peace and speaks out against war, it is not invading the purely political domain, but is keeping within the sphere of its moral and religious mission. In fact, if it did not do so, it would be betraying the Gospel of Jesus, which proclaims, "Blessed are the peacemakers," because "they will be called children of God" (Mt. 5:9). For Jesus, men and women are brothers and sisters to one another, because they are children of the heavenly Father; and so the whole notion of the "stranger" and the "enemy" that lies at the root of the ideology of war has been overcome. In its public statements and actions, the Church is only driving home the

Gospel's message of the brotherhood and sisterhood of all people.

The Church condemns war and wants peace. But what do "fighting war" and "wanting peace" mean for the Church today? "Fighting war" means fighting the ideology of war. In practice this means fighting the idea that war can solve the problems which conflicts are based on. It means fighting the notion of war as the *extrema ratio,* because in practice there is no *extrema ratio.* It is impossible to prove that all the means of avoiding war have been thought out and put into action, especially since the person who decides that war is the only remaining option is the one who out of self-interest has already determined to wage it and is merely waiting for the right moment to start it. Fighting war means fighting the notion that war is "necessary" or "inevitable," and that peace is not possible. Fighting war means, finally, fighting the idea that wars are waged for noble motives, to inaugurate a universal order of justice and peace or simply to repair injustice. Because, for the most part, these noble motives—which can be found in some people—serve others as a legal and moral smoke screen for the real motives of wars: political domination and economic interest. Fighting the ideology of war means working to unmask war, showing what it really is and what its driving energies and results are —showing, among other things, that the ones who pay for war are always the poor and the weak, whether they wear a military uniform or form part of the civilian population.

Still, the Church is not satisfied with condemning war; it wants peace. But what peace? Not the peace based on injustice, on violence, on terror, on mutual mistrust, but the peace based on justice, on solidarity, on mutual trust. The Church believes there can be no peace as long as we still have conditions of grave injustice, where men and women's just aspirations to freedom, to self-determination, to a homeland, and to a life worthy of human beings are violently denied; where feelings of frustration, hatred, and revenge among peoples, nations, and continents are fed and fueled; where mutual trust is lacking and peace is founded on the "balance of terror," on an unstoppable race toward more armaments, whether conventional or nuclear. That is why the Church speaks out decisively for peace and against every war. That is why it calls for remedying the situations of injustice that exist in the world today and that are harbingers of future wars—especially the radical injustice of the dramatically increasing poverty in the southern part of the planet.

This condition of the poor countries cannot be cured unless, among other things, we put a limit to the production of arms, whose cost has become unimaginable. To mention only a few weapons systems used in the Gulf War: a Tomahawk missile costs $1.25 million; a Patriot antimissile costs $1 million; an F-14 Tomcat fighter-bomber costs $50 million; a Tornado costs $58 million; an AWACS radar aircraft costs $100 million; a Stealth fighter plane costs $108 million; an Apache helicopter costs $10 million; an Abrams M-1 tank costs $4.17 million; a Challenger tank costs $8.3 million. We are looking at the squandering of immense amounts of money that could and should be used to eliminate the poverty of millions of people now dying of hunger.

We must heal the sore points of injustice, some of which are particularly explosive, such as the situations of the Lebanese, the Palestinians, the Kurds, and the Cypriots, and the problem of security for the state of Israel. On March 4, 1991, as he opened the meeting in the Vatican of the Catholic patriarchs and the presidents of episcopal conferences from countries caught up in the Gulf crisis, John Paul II reminded his audience that "peace and justice go hand in hand," and that there will be "just and lasting" peace in the Mideast only if the following goals are attained: genuine respect for the principle of the territorial integrity of states, the resolution of the Lebanese and Palestinian problems, and the regulation of arms sales, with disarmament treaties for the region. In reality peace has *not* returned to the Middle East with the allies' victory over Iraq. Peace will have to be patiently built up through negotiations that meet all the just demands of the peoples in the area. It must be a peace, therefore, in justice, in solidarity, in reciprocal trust—a peace that eliminates political and social oppression, forms of imperialism, and economic exploitation. Building such a peace is an enormous enterprise, but it is the only way to prevent the war in the Gulf from becoming just the beginning of an interminable series of horrors.

APPENDIX TWO

A Chronology of the Persian Gulf War

July 25, 1990: U.S. Ambassador April Glaspie tells President Saddam Hussein of Iraq that the United States has "no opinion on . . . Arab-Arab conflicts, like your border disagreement with Kuwait."

August 2, 1990: Iraq invades Kuwait. The United Nations Security Council condemns the invasion and demands the immediate and unconditional withdrawal of Iraqi forces.

August 5, 1990: President Bush says of the invasion, "This will not stand, this aggression against Kuwait."

August 6, 1990: The Security Council approves comprehensive economic sanctions against Iraq.

August 8, 1990: President Bush announces the deployment of American troops and aircraft to defensive positions in Saudi Arabia.

November 8, 1990: The President announces an increase in the number of troops (to a half million) and in equipment in order to provide for an "offensive military option."

November 15, 1990: The National Council of Churches of Christ criticizes the Bush Administration for its "reckless rhetoric and imprudent behavior" and states "unequivocally" its opposition to the buildup of troops in the Gulf.

November 15, 1990: Archbishop Daniel Pilarczyk, president of the National Conference of Catholic Bishops, writes President Bush; his letter reviews the Gulf conflict to that time in light of the church's just war criteria and states, "I fear that, in this situation, moving beyond the deployment of military forces in an effort to deter Iraqi aggression to the undertaking of offensive military action could well violate these criteria, especially the principles of proportionality and last resort."

November 27–28, 1990: The U.S. Senate Armed Services Committee hears testimony on the effectiveness of the economic sanctions.

November 29, 1990: The Security Council sets a deadline of January 15, 1991, for the withdrawal of Iraqi forces from Kuwait; also, the Security Council authorizes member states of the United Nations "to use all necessary means" to force Iraqi compliance.

November 30, 1990: The Senate Armed Services Committee hears testimony from Gary Milhollin, director of the Wisconsin Project on Nuclear Arms Control, that "there is no real short-term risk of an Iraqi nuclear weapon—at least based on what the Bush administration has told us so far." In the preceding days the Bush administration had claimed that Iraq might produce a nuclear weapon within six months to a year. (On October 3, 1991, David Kay, the leader of a U.N. team inspecting Iraq's nuclear capabilities, said Iraq could have been as little as two months away from obtaining a nuclear bomb when the war broke out. His view was contested by the U.N.'s International Atomic Energy Agency, which claimed it would have taken Iraq nearly two years to make one bomb.)

December 3, 1990: The Union of American Hebrew Congregations states that the use of military force against Iraq is "an acceptable moral option" after other means of resolving the crisis have been fully explored.

December 19, 1990: Amnesty International reports widespread abuses of human rights by Iraqi forces within Kuwait.

January 9, 1991: U.S. Secretary of State James Baker and Iraqi Foreign Minister Tariq Aziz meet in Geneva and fail to find a resolution to the crisis.

January 12, 1991: The U.S. Congress adopts a joint congressional resolution authorizing the use of American military forces in order to evict Iraq from Kuwait in accordance with Security Council resolutions.

January 13–15, 1991: Saddam Hussein rebuffs last-minute conciliation efforts by United Nations Secretary-General Javier Perez de Cuellar and the French government.

January 16, 1991: "The liberation of Kuwait has begun," the White House announces as allied forces begin air and missile attacks on Iraqi forces.

January 18, 1991: Iraq launches Scud missile attacks against Israel.

January 28, 1991: President Bush says of the liberation of Kuwait, "The first principle of a just war is that it support a just cause. Our cause could not be more noble."

February 15, 1991: President Bush calls for a popular uprising within Iraq against Saddam Hussein.

February 22, 1991: The White House demands the immediate withdrawal of Iraqi forces by the following day.

February 23, 1991: Iraq ignores the ultimatum. The ground war begins with rapid allied advances and the capture of thousands of Iraqi troops.

February 27, 1991: With remaining Iraqi units trapped near Basra, President Bush orders a cease-fire. Later General H. Norman Schwarzkopf, the commander of the allied forces, says that "historians are going to argue . . . forever" over the decision to cease fighting before the trapped remnants of the Iraqi army were destroyed. Hussein later uses these troops and equipment to suppress rebellions by the Kurds in northern Iraq and the Shiites in the south.

ABOUT THE
AUTHORS

Jean Bethke Elshtain is Centennial Professor of Political Science and Professor of Philosophy at Vanderbilt University in Nashville, Tennessee. She is the author of *Women and War* and, coming out this year, *Antigone's Daughters.* She writes on the history of political thought, contemporary political and social theory, moral philosophy, and women's studies.

Stanley Hauerwas is Professor of Theological Ethics at Duke University in Durham, North Carolina. He is the author of *A Community of Character: Toward a Constructive Christian Social Ethic* and *The Peaceable Kingdom.* His writing focuses on an ethic of virtue or character.

Sari Nusseibeh is the director of the Jerusalem Center for Strategic Research and Professor of Philosophy at Bir Zeit University in the West Bank. He is author with Mark Heller of *No Trumpets, No Drums: A Two-State Settlement of the Israeli-Palestinian Conflict.*

Michael Walzer is the U.P.S. Foundation Professor of Social Science at the Institute for Advanced Study in Princeton, New Jersey. A writer on social ethics, he is the author of *Just and Unjust Wars* and, most recently, *The Company of Critics.*

George Weigel is president of the Ethics and Public Policy Center in Washington, D.C., and a Catholic theologian specializing in social ethics. He is author of *Tranquillitas Ordinis: The Present Failure and Future Promise of American Catholic Thought on War and Peace.*

La Civiltà Cattolica is a Jesuit magazine published in Rome. Its editorials, which are written by an anonymous board of editors, are reviewed by the Vatican Secretariat of State, according to the Catholic News Service, the official press arm of the United States Catholic Conference. The director of *La Civiltà Cattolica,* the Rev. GianPaolo Salvini, S.J., said, "We are neither an official nor a semiofficial voice of the Vatican. But according to . . . tradition, we are used to working in syntony with the Holy See, and we avoid publishing articles which are contrary to the mind of the Vatican. This was the case for this editorial too."

David DeCosse is an editor at Doubleday. He is a graduate of Harvard College and the Columbia University Graduate School of Journalism.